The

ACCOUNTABILITY
FACTOR

THE BUCK **STARTS** HERE

The
ACCOUNTABILITY
FACTOR

THE BUCK **STARTS** HERE

Alan M. Dobzinski, MCC

with Margaret E. Wilson

Sweet Pea Press
Baltimore, Maryland

Dobzinski, Alan M., with Margaret E. Wilson

The Accountability Factor: The Buck Starts Here / Alan M. Dobzinski with Margaret E. Wilson

Library of Congress Cataloging-in-Publication Data is available on request.

ISBN 0-9778931-0-3

First edition
Cover design by Jim Weems, www.JimWeems.com
Text layout by Ad Graphics, Inc.
Printed in the United States of America

Phone Orders: QP Distribution, 1-888-281-5170
Author Contact: AlanD@tandem-partners.com

To my loving daughter Lauren,
I'll always love you, "no matter what."

A.M.D.

Contents

List of Tables, Figures and Sidebars

Let's Make a Deal

Some of you might remember, or may have heard of the once popular TV game show, *Let's Make A Deal*. The host, Monty Hall, would select contestants from the studio audience to participate in three or four deals, plus the "Big Deal of The Day."

"Do you want what's in the box, or what's behind the curtain?" Monty would ask. Sometimes, when a contestant would choose the curtain, Monty would offer to buy it back. "I'll give you $1,000 *not* to take the curtain!" he'd say. The decisions were always nerve-wracking and suspenseful for both contestants and the audience.

Near the end of the show, Monty would ask contestants if they wanted to keep what they had, or trade it for a chance at the "Big Deal" behind Door Number One, Door Number Two or Door Number Three. Would it be a brand new car or a lifetime supply of Jiffy Pop popcorn? A first-class trip to Hawaii or a makeshift stable complete with a live mule? On *Let's Make a Deal*, the contestants' anxious deliberations were part of the drama, the reason we wanted to tune in.

As unbelievable as it sounds, some people approach real life with the same degree of guesswork as those game show contestants. As they wake up, get dressed, make coffee, and drive to work, they worry: "Will my people all show up for work today? What new crisis will I have to handle?" And they wonder: "Should I deal with that problem employee, or should I just let it go and see what happens?" They mentally cross their fingers, cast their lots, and hope for the best.

If you're a manager in business, chances are there have been times when you, too, felt anxious about what awaited you behind your office doors. There may have been times when you dreaded going in to work, or felt resigned to dealing with the same problems over and over. Or perhaps you felt discouraged, because you couldn't seem to achieve the results you desired and others expected. We've all felt that way at times.

But if you're a manager in business, or you'd like to be, I'm here to say that you don't have to leave your results to chance. If you've ever felt anxious or confused about how to achieve better business results, this book was written for you.

It represents many hours of work we've done at Tandem Partners over the years. It explains a principle, borne out in my own experience, as well as in my coaching work with many companies over the last decade.

That principle is this: **The key to achieving better business results is accountability.**

That's why we called this book *The Accountability Factor*. A factor is something that contributes to something else, or influences the results. And what I've discovered through my work with hundreds of business owners, executives and managers, is that accountability—holding yourself and others accountable—has the greatest impact on whether you achieve your desired results.

Now you might be thinking, "Well, aren't there other factors that impact my results? Like what kind of business

I'm in, whether I use the latest technology, or know what my competitors are doing?" Of course! All of those things and more contribute to your results. *But people make it happen.* No matter what business you're in, whether it's printing or professional services, hospitality or health care, if you're a manager, you're in the people business.

Without people—and good, respectful relationships between those people—you won't get the business results you're looking for. Fortunately, this book will help you develop those relationships, so that the people who work for you and with you will *want* to be accountable. They'll *want* to produce results—for themselves and for you.

There's a way to hold people accountable that makes them eager to come to work and eager to perform.

There's a way to hold people accountable that enhances trust and respect between managers and employees.

There's a way to hold people accountable that helps them come together as a team and produce the right results, no matter what.

These ideas are at the heart of what we call The Accountability System—a professional, respectful, and effective method of getting things done and achieving results.

When you fully understand The Accountability System and the powerful, accountable relationship that every manager can have with his or her employees, your work will begin to take on new meaning. Your business results will begin to soar.

So, let's make a deal. To help you improve communication, enhance relationships, and achieve the performance you want, I'm going to provide you with useful information, presented in an engaging manner. I'll present The Accountability System using an effective combination of real life examples, stories, and advice.

In Part One of this book, you'll learn what accountability means and why it's important. In Part Two, you'll discover how to create a culture of accountability, starting with you and your team. And in Part Three, you'll gain some specific tools for becoming a great coach-manager and I'll show you how to get started.

Feel free to read one, two or all three parts of this book. As you read, don't hesitate to highlight important sections. Place sticky notes on the segments you'd like to return to later. Write ideas in the margins about how you might apply The Accountability System in your life. Send me an email or drop me a line letting me know what's working well for you.

To win the "Big Deal," however, you must begin applying the principles and practices of accountability right away. If you do, you'll start to achieve results in your work that you never before thought possible.

The Accountability System is a way of doing business, and even a way of doing life. I'm eager to share it with you, and to hear how it works for you. Let me introduce the concept by telling you about my first accountability coach.

PART ONE

Stepping Up To The Plate

CHAPTER ONE

Lessons from a Baseball Coach

"Coaching is a profession of love.
You can't coach people unless you love them."

– Eddie Robinson, Former head football coach,
Grambling State University

I don't remember his real name, but I remember that he had a big laugh and a huge passion for baseball. And for kids. He must have had a job somewhere in our working class neighborhood in Hartford, Connecticut in the late 1950s. Maybe he was a house painter, or a plumber, or a bus driver. I don't know what he did when he wasn't with us.

All I knew—and all I cared about—was that when someone asked for a volunteer to coach a group of young boys, a big man with a big laugh stepped forward.

We called him Mr. G.

The team was known as a Farm Team, for boys still a year too young for Little League. It was my first "real" baseball experience.

I'd been waiting for this for years. By the time I was four years old, I was already playing baseball by myself in our front yard. I'd toss the ball up in the air, heave the bat off my shoulder, take a swing, and jump for joy when I connected. I'd chase the ball, pick it up, and stop right there to take another swing, aiming the ball across the yard in another direction. There were no bases, no gloves, no innings, and no teammates. But by age four, I was already in love with baseball.

I collected baseball cards. I made up my own leagues, with their own teams. I watched Major League games on TV. I tried to imitate the players. I had permanent scabs on my hands and knees and elbows from teaching myself to slide.

Our family lived in Connecticut, and we were fans of the New York Giants. In 1957, the year I was nine, my father took my younger brother and me to the Polo Grounds to see Willie Mays play one last game before the team moved to the West Coast. I'll never forget sitting in the stands and hearing the crack of the bat, the roar of the crowd, and the flight of the ball as it soared up and up and up... and it's gone! Yes! Willie Mays hit a home run! It seemed everyone in the stadium rose to their feet in one huge wave of emotion. What an incredible experience it was.

So do you think I was eager to play on that Farm Team? You bet I was. I'd have a real baseball cap and a real uniform and real teammates.

And a real coach. Which is why I'm telling you this story. I want you to be a great coach, too. Not an executive coach like me, necessarily, but an in-house coach-manager who holds people accountable for getting results. This book is filled with tips, tools and techniques that will help you do just that.

First, let me tell you a little more about Mr. G., because he inspired me, and because he offers a good starting point for talking with you about accountability.

As a young boy, I had the good fortune to be coached by the kind of person who would have made a great corporate leader. Mr. G. knew his stuff. He must have played baseball as a boy, maybe even in high school. Somehow, he knew how to hold a bat and when to bunt and what to do when you're on third and the score is tied in the ninth inning with one out and the batter hits a fly ball to the outfield. (Tag up and run like heck.)

> **Show up on time, show up *every* time, and show up ready to play.**

Mr. G. knew the value of discipline. He established standards that laid the foundation for success: Show up on time, show up *every* time, show up ready to play ball. He set clear goals, expected us to achieve them, and worked hard to help us develop our skills. He treated us with respect and asked for our opinions. "See where their shortstop is standing, Alan? Do you think he's in the right position?" In return, we respected him, even revered him.

Mr. G. knew kids. He knew how to lean over and talk to us, quietly and patiently, with a sober tone that conveyed how important baseball was—to him and to us. By taking baseball seriously, he helped us to take ourselves seriously, and to commit ourselves to achieving our goals.

And he always let us be kids. So when Chris Romano found a worm and dropped it into Davey Shaffer's glove, and Davey shrieked when he discovered it, Mr. G. laughed along with the rest of us.

When we messed up, Mr. G. didn't yell. He didn't scream. He never called us names, or threw down his cap in anger, as we saw other coaches do.

Mr. G. explained how and why we goofed, and insisted that we try again. He never raised his voice and he never made us feel wrong or bad about our mistakes.

In fact, his instruction only made us more eager to learn. "Oh Alan, I know you can do better than *that*," he'd say. And when he said it, I knew it was true.

His confidence gave us confidence, and helped us step up to the plate. It takes courage to step into the batter's box, especially when you struck out last time... and the time before. But when someone believes in you, you develop the courage to try again, try harder, and improve.

I enjoyed practices as well as the games. That wasn't necessarily true for me later on in my baseball career, on other teams. With Mr. G., I felt motivated, excited, inspired. Because of his strict rules, I *had to* come to practice—but I went because I really *wanted* to—and that made all the difference.

And so it is, as you've probably noticed, with executives, managers and professional leaders of all types. The successful ones know their stuff. They take the game seriously, but not themselves. They set clear goals and enforce strict discipline, but their people want to come to work, want to produce, want to succeed.

Successful leaders love people the way Mr. G. loved kids. Genuine affection shines through in all of their interactions. They smile, they laugh, they listen respectfully to their employees. And when those employees make mistakes, effective leaders notice, comment, and correct in a way that's helpful rather than humiliating, supportive rather than stifling.

Mr. G. was a real person, not just a convenient illustration of my point. Because he was a real person, he wasn't perfect. No one is. Maybe he didn't visit his grandmother very often. Maybe he forgot to pay his bills on time, or wiped his nose on his sleeve. I wasn't focused on Mr. G.'s particular weaknesses, because his strengths were so much more memorable and so influential in my own young life.

You're a real person and so am I, and therefore, we're not perfect, either. We're going to make mistakes, and forget to do things. When interacting with the people we supervise, we won't always respond with the correct tone of voice. We won't always plan well, or say exactly the right thing.

But I share the Mr. G. story with you because he showed me, at an early age, and in a very real and tangible way, how to hold people accountable for their own success. The lesson I took away from that Farm Team year with Mr. G. was that accountability is important: *If you want to succeed, you have to show up on time, show up every time, and show up ready to play.*

Since then, I've learned that there is a way to hold people accountable that preserves dignity and creates mutual respect. I've learned that there is a way to hold people accountable that improves relationships. And achieves results. And transforms what could be a *have-to* experience into a *want-to* experience. And that makes all the difference.

It's that method, that process of holding people accountable, that most interests me now.

For the past decade, I've been coaching executives, managers and other professionals. I've been teaching them that accountability is important—though most of them already know that—and that there's a system, a process, a way of achieving results that can be learned, just as baseball can be learned.

> **As with baseball, learning to hold others accountable takes practice.**

As with baseball, learning to hold others accountable takes practice. As with baseball, accountability is a team game.

Guess who's the coach? You are.

I urge you to claim your leadership role and actively, effectively, and consistently coach your players to be accountable.

In this book, as I share with you The Accountability System, I'll encourage you to practice with your employees and with your family and friends.

I'll ask you questions, since I want you to think through how The Accountability System will work for you. Just as I respect the people who work with me, I respect you and your experiences and insights. I hope you use my suggestions, apply your own ideas, and come up with ways to implement accountability that work best for you, given your unique situation.

As you begin to see how these accountability principles apply in your life, I urge you to discuss them with the people closest to you: your staff members, your supervisor, your friends, your family. I also encourage you to send me your ideas and questions. That way, I'll be part of your team, and so will many others.

Like Mr. G., I enjoy coaching and teaching. Every once in a while, I remember my Farm Team days and I just can't help but smile at my memories of bats, bunts, baseball, and Mr. G.

Thanks, Coach!

CHAPTER TWO

What Is Accountability, Anyway?

"It is not only what we do, but also what we do not do, for which we are accountable."

– Molière (1622-1673), French
comedic actor and playwright

As a business leader, your performance is based on the performance of your people. It's based on your character, too, and on your competence, your conversations, and the way you dress, eat lunch, and shake hands. But primarily, your performance is based on whether your people perform according to the standards and results you've established.

You might sometimes wish this were not so. But it is. Regardless of the other responsibilities you have, if you're a manager, you're responsible for how two, four, six, eight, or twelve other people do their jobs. And your performance will be evaluated in light of theirs.

This raises a fundamental question: How can you ensure that those people perform?

Well, you can hire carefully. You can train thoroughly and repeatedly. You can invest in equipment and other resources. But how exactly can you help Tony and Tara and

Natalya and the rest of your team do what they're supposed to do?

By coaching them to be accountable.

> When you coach someone to *be* accountable, you include that person in the process.

"Holding them accountable" is the way we typically hear this phrase. I use it that way myself sometimes. But "holding them accountable" can sound like something a boss does *to* an employee. When you coach someone to *be* accountable, you include that person in the process. You design solutions together. And ultimately, you succeed together. Not because you have "held them" accountable, but because you've created a Want-To culture, rather than a Have-To culture.

Definitions of Accountability

Before we talk about how to create a Want-To culture, and exactly how The Accountability System works, let's ask this question: What does "accountable" mean?

Webster's Online Dictionary (2006) defines *accountable* this way:

1) Liable to be called to account: "you are answerable for this debt."
2) Being obliged to answer to an authority for your actions: "the court held the parents accountable for their minor child's acts of vandalism."

The root word—*account*—usually refers to a sum of money deposited in a bank, or a statement of debits and credits during a particular fiscal period. So it's not surprising that the first definition is financial in nature.

And how interesting that the second definition of *accountable* uses vandalism in its example. Indeed, people often associate accountability with blame and guilt, if not downright criminal activity. "Who's accountable? Fess up!" Because of these definitions, the word accountability sometimes conjures up negative images involving guilt, blame, and financial fraud. When we read this headline—"Massive Accounting Fraud Hits Wall Street Again as Another CEO is Arrested"—we wonder: Will this CEO be held *accountable* for his *accounting* activities? Maybe, maybe not. But along the way, the concept of accountability appears to have become tarnished.

Here's another example. In the weeks and months after Hurricane Katrina, national attention was fixed on the widespread devastation. The word "accountable" came up over and over again. Journalists, politicians, and pundits asked, "Who should be accountable for this catastrophe?" Clearly, they said, nature alone was not to blame.

The hurricane wreaked havoc in Mississippi and Louisiana, demolishing houses, power lines, bridges, boats, and casinos. After the levees in New Orleans broke, 80 percent of the city was immersed in filthy water sometimes two stories high. Thousands of people were stranded on rooftops, in attics, on freeway overpasses, and in Louisiana's Superdome and Convention Center. Four days passed before supplies of food and water were widely available. Four days passed before National Guard troops arrived to rescue stranded citizens and assist in the evacuation of many thousands of newly homeless people.

The economic impact from the hurricane and the burst levees was estimated at $250 billion, making it the most expensive disaster in United States history. The death toll exceeded one thousand, with more than one million people displaced. Never before in our nation's history have so many people been impacted by a natural disaster on this scale.

Reporters demanded to know: "Who should be held accountable?" Was the delayed response FEMA's fault? Within two weeks of the disaster, FEMA's director, Michael Brown, resigned. A few days later, President Bush responded to reporters' demands for accountability by saying, "Let's not play the blame game."

> **Accountability should be established and implemented early. It should not focus on finding fault or assessing blame after the fact.**

But that single resignation, followed by that simple presidential statement, did not assuage the demand for accountability. What about Homeland Security, which oversees FEMA? What about Congress and the White House, which allocate funding? Should we blame local officials, mayors or governors? Or was bureaucracy itself the problem?

Regardless of what answers emerge over time, this is the tenor of public "accountability" discussions. Though this natural disaster was unprecedented for Americans, the post-disaster response was quite typical. People focused on faultfinding, and on blame. They asked, "Whose head should roll?"

No wonder accountability gets a bad reputation. Who would want to be held accountable, if it might result in decapitation?

None of us are in a position to judge FEMA, or President Bush, or local officials for their response in the aftermath of Hurricane Katrina. However, we point to this example, because the same kinds of conversations happen within organizations when things go wrong. After human-made corporate disasters, people suddenly start talking about accountability.

The problem is, *after* the disasters, it's rather *late* for such discussions.

Accountability should be established and implemented early. It should not focus on finding fault or assessing blame after the fact. When you decide beforehand who needs to be accountable for what, and when you practice accountability on a daily basis, disasters on any scale are far less likely to happen.

Here's my definition of accountability:

The ability and willingness to follow through on your own promises and commitments.

The ability... Accountability is a skill. It requires learning, practice, implementation, revision. That's why you need a system for creating accountability. It's not the kind of thing you can learn once and for all. It's a process. As with other skills, the more you do it, the more proficient and effective you become.

...and willingness... This refers to the effort, the discipline of accountability. It requires intention. It's about showing up and taking care of business, even if you don't feel like it. The word willingness also points to the *have-to* versus *want-to* dynamic. Ultimately, accountability only happens when people want to do a good job.

...to follow through... Accountability is an ongoing effort, not a one-shot deal. That's why regularly scheduled accountability coaching is so important. That's why The Accountability System includes an organized approach, a reporting and check-in structure, and other tools to help you follow through effectively.

...on your own promises... The word promise has emotional resonance. It's the kind of word you use when you're in a trusting relationship, or a relationship in which you want to establish trust. We tend to say, "I promise," when our own integrity is on the line. We say it to people we care about. It's a demonstration of faith. It's about taking ownership. It answers the question: When it comes right down to it, will people do what they say they'll do? Can they be trusted?

...and commitments. Unlike promises, commitments may be strictly business-related. In a business context, "commitments" suggests logical, rational goals focused on performance and the bottom line: "How many new customers will you commit to bringing in this month?" Together, promises and commitments cover the scope of things you say you'll do.

DEFINITION OF ACCOUNTABILITY				
The ability...	*and willingness...*	*to follow through...*	*on your own promises...*	*and commitments.*
Skill	Effort	Ongoing	Emotional	Rational
Practice	Discipline	Regular	Trust	Business
Proficient	Intention	Scheduled	Relationship	Job Description
Effective	Want to	Organized	Ownership	Goals

So accountability is not just a question of who is liable after something goes wrong. It's not simply about who is answerable, as the dictionary says, or about feeling obliged. It's more than that.

To have true accountability, you need both ability and willingness. You need specific promises and commitments. And you need follow-through: an ongoing process of showing up and saying, "Yes, I will," over and over again.

Now at this point you might be worried. You probably wanted this book to teach you how to make *them* accountable. You might be hoping your employees' behavior will change so that their lack of accountability won't be such a problem. Don't worry, we'll get there.

But for now, here's what I want you to remember: One small change in *your* behavior can make a tremendous difference in your *team's* results. That's why the Buck **Starts** Here—with you.

If you want to hold others accountable, you must hold yourself accountable first. And wouldn't it be a good idea to offer your employees a role model of accountability, so that they can learn from you how to do it well? The Accountability System offers you just that: the building blocks for holding yourself and others accountable for results.

Recently, I met with a company to talk about The Accountability System. During our conversation, Bill, the CEO, described how at one time, the company conducted monthly "brown bag" sessions for employees. Rotating leaders would share information and facilitate discussions about how things could improve.

"What would happen?" I asked Bill.

"Oh, we'd talk, and we'd hear so many great ideas," he said.

"Then what would happen?"

"Then we would leave."

"*Then* what would happen?"

"Then we would come back next month, and share more great ideas."

Unfortunately, those great ideas went nowhere, because there was a lack of follow up. A lack of action. A lack of accountability.

That's what's missing in most organizations: a systematic approach to accountability. People talk about accountability. They hold meetings and take notes. But they don't implement a system to ensure that accountability happens routinely and predictably.

Without accountability, businesses fail. It's as simple as that. And accountability doesn't happen automatically, or in a vacuum, or once and for all.

Accountability is an ongoing process that needs structure, a system, and a leader—you—to create and enforce that system.

What are *you* going to take responsibility for?

CHAPTER THREE

Two Visions of Ultimate Accountability

*"A good coach will make his players see
what they can be rather than what they are."*

– Ara Parseghian, former University of
Notre Dame head football coach

Door Number One

Imagine that you come to work one day and there's nothing on your desk. There's nothing in your inbox. No new emails. No one has made any new demands on your time.

All of your employees are in their offices, contentedly doing their jobs. When they see you, they don't avoid you. They smile, deliver the results you're looking for, and return to work.

When you check the budget, you notice you're in the black, and well above projections.

You can't remember when you last had a disciplinary problem. Want to play golf? Need to catch up on a few errands?

> Your people don't have to resent you, or fear you, or give you blank stares when you ask them to handle something.

No problem. Everyone knows what to do, and how to do it well.

This is a fantasy. Companies don't run themselves. The people you supervise need you to be present, to pay attention, to answer their questions, and to guide them toward success.

But this fantasy can come true to some extent. Your people don't have to resent you, or fear you, or give you blank stares when you ask them to handle something. They can accomplish what you want them to. In a pleasant manner. And on time.

All you need to do is make some small changes in the way you do things. A little change in your behavior can make a big difference in your results.

All you need to do is implement The Accountability System.

Door Number Two

Now let me ask you to indulge in another fantasy. Imagine that you come to work one day and your own supervisor greets you with a smile. So far, so good. There's no ulterior motive. Your supervisor just happens to like you, and care about you, and wants you to do well and be well.

When you and your supervisor sit down for your regularly scheduled accountability coaching session, he or she begins by asking about your golf tournament, or your child's musical performance, or your spouse's recent illness. You openly share celebrations, pride, concerns, fears. You know your supervisor cares about you as a person.

As the subject easily and naturally shifts to business, you proudly report your success on a recent project, and receive warm and sincere praise in return. Next, you share some concerns you have about an important, upcoming deadline. Your supervisor listens to your concerns, encourages you to explore some new approaches and supports your decision to reprioritize some other projects in order to meet the deadline.

You also talk about your concerns related to time management, work overload, and a desire for more exercise. Your supervisor is not only empathetic, but also helpful. Together, the two of you map out some steps you can take to achieve a better work/life balance, take better care of your body, and enjoy more free time.

If you're like most people, this sounds like fiction, or downright nonsense. But it could be true.

Here's how. You can make *yourself* into this sort of person, and become the kind of supervisor described here: caring, supportive, effective. By doing so, you'll give your employees a gift. More importantly, you'll give yourself a gift: your people will achieve what you want them to achieve—willingly, and on time.

> **A little change in your behavior can make a big difference in your results.**

If you're lucky, your entire company will adopt The Accountability System, so that you and your supervisor will learn together how to become coach-managers.

But even if you're the first one to implement The Accountability System, your impact will not be limited to your employees. Because of your team's success and the obvious improvement in morale, your own boss will likely notice what you're doing and become curious. He or she may be inspired to experiment with some of your techniques.

What's behind Door Number Three, you ask? With The Accountability System, there's no need to guess! Behind

Door Number Three is *your* vision of ultimate accountability.

All you need to do is make a few changes in the way you do things. A little change in your behavior can make a big difference in your results. All you need to do is implement The Accountability System. Just open the door and walk right through it.

CHAPTER FOUR

Principles, Practices and Promises

"Leadership is lifting a person's vision to higher sights, the raising of a person's performance to a higher standard, the building of a personality beyond its normal limitations."

– Peter F. Drucker (1909-2005),
influential business thinker, author and educator

The Three Principles of The Accountability System

Principle #1:

As a leader in business, your performance is based on the performance of your people.

(You probably already knew that.)

Principle #2:

A small change in your behavior can make a big difference in your team's results.

(If you haven't noticed that yet, you're in for a pleasant surprise.)

Principle #3:
Performance improves with regular, ongoing, accountability coaching.

(Practice makes perfect.)

These are the fundamental beliefs on which The Accountability System rests. Everything else you'll learn about The Accountability System proceeds from these three principles. Of course, there's a big difference between principles and practice, between knowing and doing. For the accountability principles to have real meaning, they must be tied to a specific set of actions. They must be put into practice.

> **Accountable leaders apply the principles of accountability in tangible ways.**

The Four Practices of Accountable Leaders

Just ask anyone who's ever wanted to water ski, or learn to play the piano, or bake a bundt cake. Attention, repetition and practice are all prerequisites to perfecting a skill.

So what do you practice if accountability is your goal?

In my experience, the most effective leaders practice these four accountable behaviors:

1) They follow through on their own promises and commitments.
2) They take responsibility for the performance of their people.
3) They review progress with their team on a regular basis.
4) They do whatever it takes to achieve results without making excuses.

Accountable leaders apply the principles of accountability in tangible ways. They act on them frequently, consistently and habitually. They *practice* the right *practices.*

The Five Promises of The Accountability System

At the end of the day, accountability must manifest itself in results. However, this book is not just *about* results, it's based *on* results. Having worked with hundreds of managers at all levels in business, I can attest to the fact that The Accountability System works. My clients can attest to that, too. They tell me that they're working smarter, their employees are happier and more productive, their personal lives are more balanced and their profits are up—in some cases, way up.

Since learning any new skill takes time, energy, and practice, you may be wondering about the payoff. With that in mind, here are five promises.

If you implement The Accountability System:

Promise #1
Morale will improve as your workplace transforms from a "Have-To" culture to a "Want-To" culture.

Promise #2
Productivity will increase—not just in the short term, but also consistently, over time.

Promise #3
Managers will spend less time correcting unacceptable work and more time focused on priorities.

Promise #4
Performance reviews will become easier for managers, more meaningful for employees, and more rewarding for both.

Promise #5

Your relationships with your employees will grow due to enhanced communication, effective team-building, and ongoing professional development.

Let's take a look at each promise in more detail.

Promise #1: Morale will improve as your workplace transforms from a "Have-To" culture to a "Want-To" culture.

You probably have at least one or two "star" employees. Think about one of these people right now. Let's call this person Jim. I'd be willing to guess that part of why Jim is such a star, and why you appreciate him so much, is that he's highly self-motivated. All of us prefer to supervise people who seem to be, by nature, extremely disciplined and conscientious.

An old Dial soap commercial comes to mind: "Aren't you glad you use Dial? Don't you wish everybody did?"

Don't you wish everyone were as motivated as Jim?

The Accountability System can actually help you change the attitude people bring to work. They'll be happier, more confident and more self-directed. Their decision-making skills will improve. They'll feel better about themselves.

This is my primary promise: When you create a true culture of accountability, employees will shift from a "have to" to a "want to" frame of mind. That "want to" mentality will be evident in the quality of their work and their relationships.

Promise #2: Productivity will increase—not just in the short term, but also consistently, over time.

Some companies spend a great deal of time and energy on goal setting, on making sure goals adhere to a certain format, or are documented in just the right way. It's as if goal setting is a singular event that magically drives productivity.

> **When people are clear about what they must do, they become more accountable.**

Yet we all know that goal setting tends to be followed by… business as usual. All those well-documented goals disappear into the file drawer or the computer, never to be seen or heard from again.

With The Accountability System, goals are co-created. They're reviewed on a regular basis, and measured, and revised. Therefore, goals are more reliably achieved, and performance improves. Because this is an ongoing system, and not a fad, The Accountability System will drive performance consistently, over time.

Promise #3: Managers will spend less time correcting unacceptable work and more time focused on priorities.

Only the most sadistic bosses enjoy dealing with employees whose performance is consistently substandard. Yet many find themselves in exactly that position and do nothing about it. The Accountability System offers you an alternative. With the right system and culture, and with attention, repetition and practice, people will be able to do what they say they'll do—and enjoy it!

Does this sound like too much to hope for? If so, think about it this way: When people are clear about what they must do, they become more accountable. When they become more accountable, their performance improves. They're spared feeling angry or frustrated by poor performance, and can devote more time to higher priorities. Managers spend less time correcting and more time leading.

Promise #4: Performance reviews will become easier for managers, more meaningful for employees, and more rewarding for both.

Based on my experience with hundreds of managers, I can assure you that The Accountability System will make it easier to implement an effective performance management program.

With The Accountability System, you'll conduct an ongoing series of discussions with your employees. By the time the "annual review" rolls around, you'll already have a record of your employee's progress and performance. There won't be any surprises. You'll know exactly where they stand, and they'll know where they stand with you.

Even better, you'll have forged a stronger, more collaborative relationship with your employees. And in that spirit, performance reviews will become a time for genuine reflection and renewed commitment, rather than a painful or tedious once-a-year chore.

Promise #5: Your relationships with your employees will grow due to enhanced communication, effective teambuilding, and ongoing professional development.

More than anything, your employees want your attention and your support. With The Accountability System, you'll routinely talk with—and listen to—your team members. You'll create an open and safe environment in which you frequently discuss a variety of subjects, and together solve problems.

And it keeps getting better! Ultimately, this will not require more time than you're currently investing in management. It may seem so at first, but because your conversations will be productive, and because they'll help create an accountability culture, your employees will become more effective, more committed, and more accountable.

They'll also respect you more. They'll appreciate you more. And as you listen to and support them, your feelings for them may change as well. It's amazing how a little attention and support can improve relationships.

For instance, I coach the owner of a sizeable business. This year, the company had a big Holiday party and I was invited to attend. During the reception, someone on the management team came up to me and thanked me for working with Barb, the owner. That was good news. Apparently Barb's behavior is changing, I thought, and at least one person has noticed.

Then another manager approached me and said the same thing. "Thank you so much," she said. "We love Barb. We've always loved Barb, but you've helped her make tremendous changes in our workplace." How gratifying!

Then another person walked up to me and said the same thing. I began to think, "Gee, is this a practical joke?" But it wasn't. Throughout the evening, employees kept telling me the same thing: They liked and appreciated Barb more now than ever before. Her behavior had positively affected her leadership, and the relationship her employees have with her.

What this sort of feedback shows me is that when a leader changes, everyone benefits. Those benefits don't stop at the company door. Even Barb's husband John approached me that evening and said, "I don't know what you and Barb have been doing, but keep it up. It's working!"

When you begin to implement The Accountability System, everyone benefits. Your employees will notice. Your spouse, friends, and family are likely to feel the ripple effects. The principles and practices of The Accountability System enhance not just business relationships, but all relationships. And when people in your life are listening to you, appreciating you... when you're achieving the results you know you can achieve, that can't help but make you believe in the benefits, too.

Chapter Five

The Challenge: Holding Yourself and Others Accountable

"There is only one corner of the universe you can be certain of improving... and that's your own self."
— Aldous Huxley (1894-1963), English novelist and critic

"I can't believe it," my client Gayle complained to me one day. "One of my salespeople told me that he would be at the big trade show downtown to make some new contacts and keep our company name out there. Well, I found out the next day that he never showed up! What made it worse was that he never bothered to tell me; I had to hear it secondhand from one of our suppliers. Shouldn't I be able to trust my people? Do I have to watch their every move? Why can't they just get their work done and do what they say they're going to do? There's something wrong with this picture!"

Indeed, something *is* wrong with this picture. Like Gayle, many managers complain that employees don't turn projects in on time; the quality of their work is substandard; their attitudes are poor. Perhaps you've experienced this yourself. Do these comments sound familiar?

- "Sorry, I was too busy."
- "You should have reminded me."
- "You didn't give it to me in time."
- "You gave me the wrong information."
- "The instructions weren't clear."
- "That's not how I usually do it."
- "I didn't know it was that important."
- "I didn't know you needed it right away."

These kinds of excuses are all symptoms of a "have-to" mentality: I'll do it only if I "have to" or if you "make me." Some people have an inability to accept responsibility for their own results. Someone else, or some circumstance, must always be at fault.

Many leaders and managers have approached me for help with just these sorts of problems. Yet when I emphasize that accountability is important (though most of them already know that), and that there is a way to achieve results through greater accountability, I hear some of those same excuses.

So what's the problem? Why is it so challenging to hold ourselves and others accountable?

Six Reasons People Don't Hold Themselves and Others Accountable

1) They don't have enough time

Most managers want better accountability, but when they learn that it will require a certain commitment on their part, they balk. They don't have time to think about it. They don't have time to plan. They don't have time to meet with their employees. They're overworked, overloaded and overwhelmed.

JOHNNY'S STORY

Early one morning, Johnny's mother knocked on his bedroom door and said, "Johnny, it's time to get up. You're going to be late for school."

"Yeah, yeah," Johnny muttered, as he rolled over and drifted back to sleep.

Some minutes later, his mother came to the door and knocked again. "Johnny," she said with concern. "It's 6:35. If you don't get up, you'll be late for school."

"Yeah, whatever," Johnny grumbled, before he promptly rolled over and went back to sleep.

Finally, his mother came to the door and called out loudly, "Johnny, get up! I mean it! You're going to be late for school!"

"I don't want to go to school," Johnny groaned.

"Why not?" his mother asked.

"The kids don't like me," Johnny whined. "The teachers don't like me either. I'm just not happy there and I don't want to go. Give me one good reason why I should."

"Well, I'll give you two good reasons," Johnny's mother snapped back. "First of all, you're 47 years old. Second, you're the principal of that school. Now you get yourself up out of that bed, be accountable, and get to school!"

This story, while humorous, is also instructive. Here we have a man who's never really grown up. He still lives at home. He depends on his mother to wake him up. Yet he also resists her authority, as children sometimes do, and comes up with excuses for not doing what he's supposed to do.

Don't we all know people like Johnny? People who've somehow managed to rise to a level of authority or influence, yet deep down, are still immature children? They don't take responsibility for their actions, they blame others for their unhappiness, and they don't keep their commitments without repeated poking and prodding.

If we're honest, we probably can all see a little of ourselves in Johnny. Some mornings, we just want to crawl under the covers and go back to sleep. Sometimes, accountability is the last thing we want to think about.

We all know the feeling. In my entire professional career, not one manager has ever said to me, "You know, Alan, I find myself with so much extra time on my hands these days. Can you give me something more to do?" In fact, quite the opposite is true. In this fast-paced world in which we live, many professionals struggle to balance competing demands on their time.

Yet I do know many people—some of them my clients—who seem to get the most out of every 24 hours. And it's not because they run around frazzled, or hire people to take care of all their personal errands, or only sleep four hours a night. It's because they've replaced some previously unproductive activities with more productive ones.

In the long run, implementing The Accountability System will actually *save* you time. So instead of allowing yourself to be overwhelmed, remember that implementing accountability will help you develop new patterns of behavior that not only will save you time, but also bring you closer to achieving your goals.

2) They don't have enough support

People in the workplace have certain expectations based on their past experiences. Therefore, they may not automatically embrace the idea of implementing a "new accountability system." It may sound like just one more hocus-pocus management program that will be forgotten within a month or two. If a company has a history of announcing new programs that never go anywhere, it may be difficult to rally the leaders, let alone the troops.

You may not even receive support from your own supervisor. After all, if you and your team start becoming super productive, everyone else may look bad by comparison. If you and your staff change, then other people—including your boss—may fear they'll have to change, too. They may even resent your success, especially if your productivity inadvertently reminds them of their own weaknesses or insecurities.

> Some mornings, we just want to crawl under the covers and go back to sleep. Sometimes, accountability is the last thing we want to think about.

"I've asked my boss for more accountability coaching," reported one manager, "but he hasn't started yet." No wonder. He probably has no idea what you're talking about and feels too embarrassed to ask. So he's taking the easier path: inaction.

3) They have bad habits

By the time someone becomes a manager, he or she is in the habit of doing things a certain way. And the truth is, it's a real challenge to change the way we do simple, everyday things like run meetings, ask people for their opinions, or listen to their answers. Change can be difficult. "It's hard to really listen to other people, and allow them the space to develop," clients tell me. "Sometimes it's just easier to tell them what to do."

Others protest, "You can't teach an old dog new tricks."

But is that always true? With the right information, the right coaching and the right tools, some "old dogs" are quite eager to learn new tricks.

Not too long ago, I was working with an executive I'll call Bob. Bob's company was implementing The Accountability System, and, being a senior leader, Bob did his best to support the initiative. However, early on, he shared with me privately that he was a bit skeptical and didn't think he needed any help with his leadership or with accountability. His team was performing well, they were hitting their goals, and his relationships with his team couldn't be any better—or so he thought.

After we had been working together for several weeks, Bob and I touched on the idea of being "fully present" with his employees. I asked Bob to take on a homework assignment. During the next two weeks, whenever Bob was meeting with one of his people, I asked him to be conscious of how fully present he was during the interaction.

The next time we met, Bob reported that the assignment had made him acutely aware of a bad habit. If an employee came to Bob's office door while he was working, Bob would respond with his back turned, while continuing to type away on his computer. When in meetings, he was continually interrupted by incoming calls to his cell phone. He wasn't fully present for those small, daily interactions. He wasn't giving his people 100 percent of his attention. And he realized that he may have been giving the impression, at times, that he was too distracted, or not interested in what his employees had to say. So Bob, an executive with 20+ years of experience and a high performing team, decided to unlearn that bad habit. And he did.

> The Accountability System is simple and effective, and its principles can become good habits rather quickly and easily.

Many other experienced people like Bob have learned to become more effective coach-managers through The Accountability System. It's simple and effective, and its principles can become good habits rather quickly and easily.

4) They have good people

Do your employees clearly understand your expectations? How do you know?

Some managers assume that because they have good people, they don't need a system for accountability. Their good people always know exactly what to do and precisely how to do it.

"Oh, Darlynn? She's amazing. She's such a great employee, I hardly spend any time at all with her."

I wonder how Darlynn feels about that.

Other managers don't hold people accountable because they're afraid of "micromanaging." Somewhere along the line, meeting with your employees and offering to help them achieve more got a bad reputation. That "micromanager" label can keep managers from spending time with the employees who deserve it most: those who already are performing.

5) They don't know what they're missing

Some managers, not understanding what accountability really is, talk a good game. "Oh, I do coaching all the time," they tell me. "I've got the bases covered."

Others, not understanding what The Accountability System really offers, say, "Well you know, we're having a pretty good year. So we must be doing okay with accountability."

In other words, they don't see the value.

But when you drill down, you often find that they're actually not all that happy with the quality of work being produced. Or things aren't getting done on time. Or morale could be better. They're not really "doing coaching," either; they just think they are, because they don't fully understand what goes into a coaching relationship. Yet they lack the vision to see how much better things could be.

And let's not forget the simple human fear of embarrassment. Who wants to start a new initiative only to fumble or fail? If you've never tried something before, you might be afraid you'll blow it. That fear can be a tremendous barrier, blocking many people from seeing what's missing and making the changes that would vastly improve their work lives.

6) They don't know what to do

Most people understand that the old style of management doesn't work anymore. Employees don't want to be "bossed around." If you try that, they're likely to go elsewhere.

People aren't limited to a "one company town" anymore; they can leave their small town and move to a bigger city. They can get more education. They can change careers. They can leave your company—and they will—if they don't like how they're being treated.

Managers understand this, but they often don't understand how to treat people differently. "I'm the boss, but I can't just tell people what to do, so how in the world can I get them to produce?"

Most people don't learn how to implement accountability when they're in school. Most of us didn't learn it from our own bosses as we were coming up in the ranks, either. Fortunately, there's The Accountability System. In my experience, only a small percentage of people who are exposed to this system find it too daunting to implement. The rest welcome the chance to make a change, and use the system to help them achieve their goals.

PART TWO

Creating A
Want-To Culture

CHAPTER SIX

The Buck Starts Here

"In reading the lives of great men, I found that the first victory they won was over themselves... self discipline with all of them came first."

– Harry S. Truman (1884-1972)
thirty-third president of the United States

To achieve accountability, you need three things:

- A culture.
- A process.
- And <u>you</u>.

Let's talk about you.

What has the greatest impact on whether people are held accountable?

You do.

What can you do to stop being frustrated by other people's lack of accountability?

You can stop focusing on other people and start focusing on yourself.

In an ideal world:

- You are accountable to yourself.
- Your employees are accountable to themselves.
- You become accountable to each other.

But someone has to go first.

I know what you might be thinking: *I'm not the one with the problem!*

I believe you. You're probably a highly motivated, dedicated and hard working professional. You might be an outstanding manager. You might excel at getting things done. So let's agree on that: You're not the problem.

However, you can be the *solution*—or a large part of it. And that's good news. If your staff is not performing up to snuff, you can change that situation *by changing the way you lead.* It begins when you take control of the accountability process.

> **If your staff is not performing up to snuff, you can change that situation *by changing the way you lead.***

Now let me say here that there's a big difference between being in control of a process and trying to control other people. I don't recommend the latter. (You'll hear a lot more about that in Chapter 10.) So as strange as it sounds for a coach to say this, you're going to take more control.

You won't always *perceive* yourself as having control, because you'll be asking for input, opinions, and even advice from your employees. Some of this will feel new, maybe uncomfortable. You'll be commanding less and cooperating more.

Your employees won't perceive you to be controlling either, because your process will be inclusive and respectful. And because you'll be taking control in an effective way—as opposed to all the other ways you may have tried in the past—your employees will produce better work. They'll feel more appreciated and understood. Paradoxically, if all goes well, they'll experience more control *themselves*—over their goals, their time, and their interaction with you.

All you have to do is be willing to make a few small changes in the way you do things.

> **Accountability needs a process, and it helps to have the right culture, but *you* have the greatest impact.**

Now this might not be what you want to hear. Often, I'm called in when companies want to improve their overall accountability, and the person who contacted me, in effect, points at his or her staff and says, "Fix them."

I'd love to help, but it just doesn't work that way. Deep down, managers know it doesn't work because that's what they (and perhaps you) have been trying to do for years: fix those other people. It didn't work because it doesn't work.

The truth is, you can't change other people. However, you do have the option of changing yourself. You might choose not to change. Many people don't *want* to change. But you do have that option.

So let me ask you: What are *you* willing to take responsibility for?

That personal responsibility is central to The Accountability System. Accountability needs a process, and it helps to have the right culture, but *you* have the greatest impact.

Now I understand if you still want to moan and groan because your production manager is disorganized, your executive assistant can't spell, and your sales staff is lazy. Fine. Go ahead. Whine away.

But when you get tired of complaining, keep in mind that you do have the power to change your situation. Not by ranting and raving at your people, but by quietly and systematically implementing a process that will hold them—and you—accountable.

When your behavior changes, accountability begins.

Becoming Accountable to Yourself

Recently, I was talking with a client named Lawrence. He and I had been working together for about a year. I asked Lawrence, "In our work together this past year, what has had the biggest impact on your business?"

"Well, I learned to be accountable to myself," he said, "and then I became more accountable to everybody else."

"Let's talk about that a bit more," I said. "How did that happen? How did you become more accountable to yourself?"

"Well, it certainly didn't happen overnight," he replied.

Lawrence admitted (as I had observed) that early on, he had trouble scheduling meetings with me, and with his employees. Lawrence likes to work alone and he doesn't like meetings. He worried about feeling foolish, or looking incompetent. I assured him that we all feel that way at times.

Fortunately, Lawrence is interested in learning. He's receptive. And that's essential. If people believe they already know everything, or even that they know enough, they may not be open to accountability coaching.

Lawrence was open to becoming accountable, for the good of his company and for his own good. But he didn't know what to do differently. So we started by working on Lawrence's own behavior, while simultaneously adding tools and techniques that he could implement in his company. The two—changing oneself and changing one's situation—work hand in hand. The Accountability System works, and here's one simple reason why.

Let's say you schedule an accountability coaching session for 8:30 a.m. on Monday morning. Your employee, Kathy, shows up on time, but you're still out at Starbucks. When you finally sit down at 8:50, how can you in good conscience discuss *Kathy's* accountability? You're going to learn how to show up on time, because you know as a leader you need to set the example.

More importantly, with The Accountability System, you'll have a structure and process for accountability. And as you learn to hold Kathy accountable, the System itself will teach you how to hold yourself accountable. You won't be perfect—no one is—but as with everything, you'll improve with practice.

In this way, by gradually making changes in his own daily practices, Lawrence became accountable to himself and others. You can, too. And that, as Lawrence discovered, is the biggest factor in overall success: a leader's willingness to go first.

Truman and the Buck

While doing research for this book, we asked a broad sampling of businesspeople to define accountability on a written survey. We were curious: When people think about accountability, what comes to mind? How do they define it? The answers fell into these seven categories:

1) The Buck Stops Here
2) The Buck Stops There
3) Personal Responsibility
4) Courageous Acceptance

5) Universal Responsibility
6) Doing Things Well
7) True to Your Word

The first category—"The Buck Stops Here"—was most popular. (For full details of the Accountability Survey, see Appendix A.)

Like our survey respondents, I'm fond of President Harry S. Truman's memorable line. In 1945, a friend of Truman's presented him with a glass sign on which the words were painted, "The Buck Stops Here!" Truman displayed it on his desk throughout the rest of his administration.

He referred to it several times in public. In an address at the National War College in December 1952, President Truman said:

> "You know, it's easy for the Monday morning quarterback to say what the coach should have done after the game is over. But when the decision is up before you—and on my desk I have a motto which says 'The Buck Stops Here'—the decision has to be made."

The concept came to define his presidency so much that he used the phrase again when leaving office in January 1953. "The President—whoever he is—has to decide," he said. "He can't pass the buck to anybody. No one else can do the deciding for him. That's his job."

The sign has been displayed at the Truman Memorial Museum and Library since 1957.

For almost 50 years, Truman's famous phrase has been a cultural touchstone of accountability. Parents tell their children about the president with the sign on his desk. Employers and politicians use the story to claim responsibility themselves. It's memorable and meaningful because so often, the opposite is true: People shirk responsibility, refuse to step up to the plate, and blame others.

Ever wonder what the "buck" was that Truman was talking about? The word "buck" comes from "pass the buck," which means forwarding responsibility to someone else.

That phrase probably originated with the game of poker. In the Wild West, a marker was used to indicate whose turn it was to deal, and a knife with a buckhorn handle was often used for that purpose. If a player did not want to deal, he could "pass the buck" to the next player.

It would be easy, and obvious, for me to recommend that you print up your own sign, and accept responsibility for what goes on in your business. If you want to do that, fine.

What I'm more interested in is where the buck *starts*. I'd like it to start with you.

What that means is for you to take responsibility first. For you to be accountable first. To model accountability for your staff. To accept final, ultimate responsibility.

The buck starts with you. Demonstrate accountability first, so that others will learn from—and *with*—you.

....

CHAPTER SEVEN

Learning to Be Accountable

*"The beautiful thing about learning
is that no one can take it away from you."*
– B. B. King, American blues guitarist and songwriter

I'm always curious about how people learn to become accountable. So on the accountability survey I referenced earlier, I posed just that question to a variety of business managers: "How do people learn to be accountable?" In response, most people identified their parents. "Plain old Midwestern, down-to-earth, do-what-you-say-you-will-do, hard-working parents," wrote one respondent.

Some thought they were born with the trait ("I came from the factory wired this way.") Others learned from friends, professional mentors, books, or seminars ("An EST-like seminar that I attended in my youth taught me the valuable lesson that we are the true and only masters of our own destiny.") For more samples of their responses, see Appendix A.

Now let me tell you my own accountability story.

As I was writing this book, I started thinking about who influenced me, and how. I want to share my story with you for two reasons:

1) It shows that learning to be accountable is an on-going process. Maybe like me, you're learning accountability relatively late in life. If so, it's *never* too late!

2) Accountability is not a solo activity. No matter how self-disciplined you are, your ability to get things done will improve when you start inviting other people to support you in becoming more accountable.

My parents were wonderful people. My mother, a home-maker, was personable and popular; she loved to laugh and have fun. She also was effective at managing money, which was fortunate, since there were six of us living on my father's modest wages as a tool and die maker. He went to trade school, but neither he nor my mother graduated from high school. They valued education as a concept, but not having received a formal education themselves, they didn't really know how to guide their children in that direction.

For the first six years of school, I felt like the perfect kid. School was natural and easy for me. I had a lot of friends. I was good at baseball. Life was great.

In seventh grade, things started to change. For one thing, schoolwork grew more demanding. I'd done so well in elementary school that the teachers placed me in honors classes. Those honors classes were a complete shock to me. I floundered, and I feared flunking out.

Meanwhile, like seventh grade boys everywhere, I started noticing girls. My response to the new academic stress and the sudden appeal of girls was to become a class clown, horsing around and rebelling like crazy. Needless to say, this did nothing for my grades.

What I needed at this point was… The Accountability System! Truly, I did. I needed someone to coach me, to help me clarify my goals, to guide me away from negative behaviors and toward success. My first baseball coach, Mr. G., had taught me some discipline, but without ongoing reinforcement, I was really struggling.

I could have used some training in organization and time management. It would have helped to have someone hold me accountable for doing my homework. Unfortunately, that didn't happen. And I continued to act out.

> **I needed someone to coach me, to help me clarify my goals, to guide me away from negative behaviors and toward success.**

It seems that my relationship with my father changed around then, too. When I was younger, we spent a lot of time together. He took me to baseball games or we played in the front yard. One of the best childhood memories I have is of my Dad coming home from work every day and how he'd greet me in the front yard and toss me up into the air. He would catch me by grabbing me under the arms and then would toss me straight up again. In the summer, the neighborhood kids would hang around in my front yard waiting for my Dad to get home so that they could have a turn being tossed in the air, too. We would make him do it over and over until he complained that his arms were too tired to continue.

But as I got older, and my "little kid" problems became "big kid" challenges, I needed to relate to my father in a different way. I needed to talk more, but I was convinced, as only a teenager can be, that no one was listening. I felt as if no one seemed to care about my perspectives, my hopes, or my problems. And I didn't know how to ask for help.

Now I know that everyone has difficulties in those teen years; I don't think my situation is all that unusual. I don't even wish my childhood were any different, because it ultimately made me who I am. I'm just telling you about my own journey because I want you to know that accountability was something I had to learn.

For me, the turning point came in my early forties. I was married, with a small child, and had owned a business for a number of years. The independent retail chain I'd started had grown to four stores and could boast several million dollars in annual sales. But that was part of my problem—boasting. In my own mind, I was doing a lot better than I actually was. My ego was out of control.

To my great surprise, a few people who cared about me gave me some strong feedback. They let me know in no uncertain terms that my behavior was controlling. It was condescending. I wanted to do everything my way. That got my attention.

I'm not proud to say that. But I'm grateful now for the feedback, as painful as it was to hear then.

Meanwhile, my marriage was heading toward divorce. I couldn't see how to keep the marriage together, yet I agonized over the impact it would have on our young daughter. It was a difficult time.

Finally, I realized I needed help. Between my marital problems and the strong feedback I had received from my family and friends, I had reached a pivotal point in my life. So one day I made an appointment to see a counselor. I don't know what I expected; I'd never sought professional help before. I guess I thought I would be lectured or shamed. Maybe in a way, I felt I deserved it. But that didn't happen. My counselor treated me with genuine compassion. "Hey, come on," she said. "Do you think you're the first person this has ever happened to?"

That was the beginning of a new outlook for me. I thought I was going to talk about my impending divorce and my daughter, but I ended up looking at myself.

I now believe that this sort of honest self-reflection is essential for accountability. The word accountability sounds clinical and practical, but it requires a certain ongoing commitment to self-awareness.

> **If you picture the kind of person who develops accountability... you'll see that it must be someone who cares about commitments, cares about relationships, and cares enough about his or her own integrity to follow through.**

If you picture the kind of person who develops accountability as I've defined it—*the ability and willingness to follow through on your own promises and commitments*—you'll see that it must be someone who cares about commitments, cares about relationships, and cares enough about his or her own integrity to follow through.

My next step toward becoming accountable was joining a group for divorced, separated and widowed men. It was a place where I could talk openly and be supported by people who knew what I was going through. The discussion was respectful. It was constructive. The men I came to know in this forum, For Men Only (or "FMO"), helped me get back on track by supporting me.

They let me know that I wasn't a Lone Ranger and didn't need to be. They helped me be accountable for the steps I planned to take. At each meeting, we would ask each other about the progress we were making. Although our discussions were informal, "going public" with my issues and concerns created a built-in accountability process. I learned a lot about how that works, and how valuable it can be.

That was more than 10 years ago, and I still get together with members of my FMO group when I'm in Connecticut. I started a similar group some years ago where I live now, in the Baltimore/Washington area. Many of us meet for dinner now and then to support each other and share what's going on in our lives.

Having gone through some painful experiences in my life, I'm now blessed with a wonderful support system. I'm in a mastermind group with other professionals who meet once a month. I meet with other speakers and trainers from the National Speakers Association on a regular basis. I have several close friends who happen to have professional training in counseling and who are superb listeners. One of these men acts as my informal business coach. Another takes regular hikes with me, where we walk and talk. It's always a fantastic conversation.

And I'm delighted to report that I have a loving and involved relationship with my daughter, who is now a teenager. She's taught me a lot about accountability. You know how outspoken teenagers can be about making sure parents do what they say they'll do!

In my life so far, I've learned accountability from a number of sources: my first baseball coach, a counselor, a men's group, and my family. I continue to learn it from my colleagues, friends and clients.

My accountability story—being humbled by divorce and parenthood, receiving honest feedback about my shortcomings, realizing I needed help, and reaching out to others—points to these truths:

1) Learning to be accountable is a lifelong process.
2) Accountability is not a solo activity. We all need other people.

CHAPTER EIGHT

The Accountability Culture: From "Have-To" to "Want-To"

"Do not go where the path may lead, go instead where there is no path and leave a trail."

– Ralph Waldo Emerson (1803-1882)
American author, poet and philosopher

As I mentioned, in order to have accountability, you need three things: a culture, a process, and you. This is the culture chapter. It's about how to create a culture of accountability: a "Want-To" culture, you might say, as opposed to a "Have-To" culture, which, unfortunately, you find in some work environments.

What exactly do I mean by "culture"? Well, basically, culture is the "personality" of an organization. It's the values and norms and assumptions of a company, as well as the behaviors of the people working in it. Culture is one of those things that's hard to express in words. But you can sense it. You can see signs of it, too, by the way people talk, or what they wear, or how the offices are arranged, just like you can get a feel for someone's personality when you meet them for the first time.

So every organization has a culture. You might not know what to call it, but it's there. And it's never neutral. The culture either supports accountability or detracts from it.

Let's look first at a Have-To Culture. You might recognize this scenario.

The boss hands out assignments. Employees must complete them, the boss explains, exactly this way and by this deadline. "Any questions?"

But the boss isn't really interested in the questions employees have, and doesn't appear to have time to answer them anyway. Therefore, few people ask questions.

Then the employees do the work... or not. They know they *have to*. But they complain about it, as they might complain about having to pay a parking ticket. Most people don't like being told what to do. They don't like working on assignments that don't feel meaningful or won't be appreciated. They don't like being "bossed around."

So they do it reluctantly. They do the minimum work required, without enthusiasm or creativity. They do it slower than it needs to be done, in order to postpone the next assignment.

And they begin to resent it. They begin to resent their work and the company. They may begin to resent the boss. That resentment may become noticeable in their attitudes, their demeanor, and the quality of their work. Eventually, the boss begins to resent *them*.

The people in a Have-To culture also reject responsibility. It was *your* assignment; they're just doing it because they *have to*. They're not committed. They're not involved. They begin to behave like irritable children: "Well, I don't want to," they might say to themselves, "but I will, because she's *making* me." All along the way, they're resisting, resenting, and rejecting responsibility.

The 7 Rs of a Have-To Culture

Clearly, there are severe consequences associated with a Have-To culture. Employees experience a range of symptoms that only get worse with prolonged exposure.

1. Reluctance: "I'm not sure we should."
2. Resistance: "I don't think I want to."
3. Resentment: "I'll do it if you make me."
4. Rage: "I'm angry about it."
5. Rebellion: "I'm not going to."
6. Revenge: "I'll make you pay for this."
7. Resignation: "I'm outta here."

So what does a Want-To culture look like? Obviously, employees want to come to work in the first place. It's not a big deal to get up in the morning, as it was for Johnny, the school principal. People in a Want-To culture arrive at work ready to work. They're eager to get started and they show genuine interest and enthusiasm for what's going on that day.

> **People in a Want-To culture work *voluntarily*, *cooperatively*, and *willingly*.**

In contrast to the 7Rs, people in a Want-To culture work *voluntarily*, *cooperatively*, and *willingly*. They feel responsible for their own success and the success of the company. They want to be there, want to perform, want to succeed.

Do those people exist? Of course!

You might be one of them. And it's quite possible that you already work in a Want-To culture.

But what if you don't? That's what The Accountability System is all about—how to transform a Have-To culture into a Want-To culture.

It starts in small ways—with you, your work group and the employees you supervise. Remember: You can't change other people, you can only change yourself. And a small change in your behavior will make a big difference in your results. So it really is up to you.

In order to create a Want-To culture, there are three choices you need to make:

1) Will I choose to supervise by attacking or approaching?
2) Will I motivate people by controlling them or caring for them?
3) Will my communication style confuse or clarify?

These three choices form the Approach–Care–Clarify, or "ACC" Model of Accountability:

A: Approach, Don't Attack

> **Keep in mind the golden rule of account-ability: Do unto others as *they* would have you do unto *them*.**

When talking with your staff about what could or should be done, keep in mind the golden rule of account-ability: Do unto others as *they* would have you do unto *them*. You see, it's about what *they* need. When you approach rather than attack, you encourage employees to be honest with you, to tell you what they need in order to do their best. Approach honestly. Discuss openly. Plan accordingly.

C: Care, Don't Control

Discover the best that each person has to offer, and capitalize on those strengths. Praise your staff for what they're doing well, so that they know they're making a positive contribution. Demonstrate that you're looking out for their personal and professional well-being. Go to bat for people, supporting them with other leaders. Will you lose control this way? Not really. By relinquishing control up front and focusing instead on expressing care and concern for your employees, you'll gain more control over yourself—and the accountability process.

C: Clarify, Don't Confuse

Establish and maintain open, honest, and regularly scheduled two-way discussions with your employees. Don't assume that you know what's on their minds. Don't assume that they can read yours. Keep people in the loop by sharing news, plans and ideas. Share your grand plan, too, so that everyone understands what the work is really all about. When employees know what they're working toward, they will tend to commit to that vision and work with you to achieve it.

THE ACC MODEL OF ACCOUNTABILITY	
"WANT-TO"	**"HAVE-TO"**
Accountable	**Not Accountable**
When I demonstrate these behaviors:	When I demonstrate these behaviors:
APPROACH	ATTACK
CARE	CONTROL
CLARIFY	CONFUSE
I create a "Want-To" culture	I create a "Have-To" culture
As a result, my people will be more likely to **ACCEPT** responsibility and they will be accountable.	As a result, my people may **REJECT** responsibility and they will not be accountable.

Approach–Care–Clarify
A+C+C = Accountability!

That's the central message of The Accountability System. And there's more to come. But when you demonstrate Approaching, Caring and Clarifying, you begin making the shift from a "Have-To" mentality to a "Want-To" mentality. Learn the ACC Model and you'll be well on your way to creating a culture of accountability.

I don't mean to imply that you can create a culture all by yourself. I hope that you're studying and implementing this system along with the rest of the leadership team at your company. I hope that all of you, together, decide to create a Want-To culture.

But even if you don't have the support of other leaders in your organization yet, you can still create a Want-To culture within your own work group. And it all starts with the ACC Model: Approach, Care, and Clarify.

. . . .

CHAPTER NINE

Approach, Don't Attack

*"Coaches have to watch for
what they don't want to see and listen
to what they don't want to hear."*

**– John Madden, former NFL head football coach,
television broadcaster and member of
the Pro Football Hall of Fame**

THE ACC MODEL OF ACCOUNTABILITY	
"WANT-TO"	**"HAVE-TO"**
Accountable	**Not Accountable**
APPROACH	**ATTACK**
CARE	CONTROL
CLARIFY	CONFUSE

"What is your problem?!"

"You totally blew the budget!"

"You should have had that report done by now!
What's taking you so long?!"

I hope you've never had a supervisor who reprimanded you
for poor performance like that. But chances are, you have.

In any case, you can imagine what it feels like to be spoken to that way. Regardless of the intent, this kind of language (especially when accompanied by expressions of disgust, disdain or disrespect), feels like an attack.

Have you ever spoken to people this way yourself? If you find yourself feeling the least bit defensive right now, you might be saying to yourself, as clients have said to me, "I'm not *attacking* my staff, I'm just *confronting* them. That's my responsibility. That's what I'm paid to do."

Unfortunately, so-called confrontations often do feel like attacks. Remember, as a manager, you're in a position of power. In a very real sense, you have your employees' futures in your hands. Your employees are vulnerable to your moods, your decisions, and your whims. Your whispers can sound like shouts to them. So when you "just confront," your employees may receive it like a blow to the head or a punch in the stomach.

Because so many clients tell me that they "just confront," I checked out the meaning of the word with a group of about 40 mid-level managers and senior executives who were implementing The Accountability System. I asked them:

"When you hear the word 'confront,' what does that mean to you?"

Problem	Dead end
Challenge	Angry
Right versus wrong	Close-minded
Embarrassment	Cornered
Intimidation	Conflict
One-way	Me against you

Aggressive	Defensive
"In your face"	Positional power
Negative	Breeds tension
Emotional	Feeling "less than"
Fight	Superiority
Accuse	Trepidation
Argument	Blame
Push back	Altercation

And that's just a small sample of their responses. What came to your mind? What does "confront" mean to you?

Note that these associations are overwhelmingly negative. One manager probably said it best: "To confront inevitably leads to confrontation. When it's happening to you, it generally feels a lot like an attack."

Like attacking, confronting comes from a "me" place. When you attack or confront, you're not taking the other person into consideration. You're not thinking about what you might have contributed to the situation, either, as you would when you come from a "we" place.

Sometimes, a manager is afraid—What will happen if this project isn't completed on time?—and takes it out on the employee. Sometimes the manager is being egocentric, thinking only of himself or herself.

But most of the time, managers aren't thinking at all. They're just reacting. Or they lack the skills to solve the problem. Or they just don't know a better way. Maybe they grew up in a home where confrontation was the norm. Maybe they learned from a manager who always confronted or attacked them.

Some people who use a confronting style shift between attacking and avoiding. These people do nothing—until they can't stand it anymore—at which time they attack.

Attacking tends to shut down creativity. Who can think when they're being attacked? Who dares submit an idea when it might be mocked or rejected out of hand? When you attack someone, you deprive them of the opportunity to grow and contribute in ways you might not realize are possible. When you attack someone, you deprive *yourself* of the opportunity to learn from them. If you assume you have the answer, you will fail to benefit from the input others might provide.

Your relationship also will be damaged, as you've probably noticed if you've ever been on the receiving end of an attacking managerial style. When people feel attacked, they stop trusting the attacker.

The truth is, a confrontational or attacking style just doesn't work. Maybe it used to, when workers had fewer options, and felt compelled to stay with one company for 30 years. But nowadays, if people don't like the way you're treating them, they'll leave. We live in a different society now, and people are more educated, more aware of their rights, and more likely to defend their dignity. They want to be treated professionally, with respect.

> **When you attack someone, you deprive them of the opportunity to grow and contribute.**

And thank goodness for that. We all want that.

Fortunately, neither attacking nor confronting is necessary for communicating effectively with your employees about mistakes, shortcomings, or other problems. Fortunately, there's a better way. It's called "Approach." Let's take a look again at what some of my clients have had to say.

"What comes to mind when you hear the word 'approach'?"

Advance	Without assumption
Come near	Proactive
Come close	Proceed
Conversation	Thoughtful
Understanding	Team
Level-headed	Friend
Unemotional	Interest
Involved	Respect
Collaborative	Honesty
Solution	Inquiry
Willingness	No blame
Openness	Trust
Seeking information	Move toward

Note that all of these words are positive or neutral. People don't seem to have negative associations with the word "approach." In some ways, the word "approach" is inquisitive and open. Granted, it's not a word you'll necessarily use out loud: "Rick, I need to approach you later this afternoon." But you probably don't say "confront" out loud, either, or "attack." These attitudes are exhibited through your behavior more than they are by your words.

When you need to have a conversation with one of your employees—even someone who's not working up to par—think of it as an approach, and you'll be starting off on the right foot: open, receptive, considerate, seeking information, interested in what the other person has to say.

Now let me ask you this: What's the quickest way to resolve a conflict or misunderstanding? Whether it's in business or a personal context, I believe the quickest way is through the truth.

When I'm delivering The Accountability System, I sometimes make that same assertion and ask the participants: "How many of you agree that the truth is the quickest way to resolve things?" They all raise their hands. Then I say: "And how many of you actually practice that?" I get some laughs, and people look around to see whose hand is still up, because we all know it's hard sometimes to tell the whole truth.

> **When you openly share the truth, it sets the stage for your people to do the same.**

It's hard to say, "Frankly, I just blew it today." Or, "I didn't include Mr. Miller in the email. I guess I was rushing too much." Or, "I got distracted by something else and I just didn't call Melinda like I was supposed to."

It's hard to take responsibility, to admit our mistakes, and to make ourselves vulnerable to other people by telling the simple truth about our human failings.

Understanding how hard it is, it's not fair for managers to expect their staff members to do it first. If you haven't established that kind of complete honesty and openness, they're not going to be the first to do so.

But a small change in your behavior can have a huge impact on your staff. When you openly share the truth—about yourself, your expectations, and your own faults and failings—it sets the stage for your people to do the same. That's the crux of the Approach philosophy: you meet respectfully, talk honestly, and work things out.

How?

Here's an example. A client of mine was planning to give a presentation to a large audience. I've seen Jon give presentations before and he's good: direct, organized, effective. But he has a few distracting habits.

Now Jon and I have an understanding about giving and receiving feedback. So as I was reviewing his material with him, I said, "Jon, I'd like to give you some feedback on your speaking style. How would you feel about that?"

That's a simple example of how to approach someone. I asked if I could give him some information that I thought would improve his presentation.

Jon is a perfectionist. It's not easy for him to hear criticism. But that's my job as his coach, or part of it: to give him honest, helpful feedback.

And that's your job as a coach-manager. When you treat your people professionally and respectfully, approaching rather than attacking, you'll be much more likely to inspire in them a desire for accountability and professional growth.

CHAPTER TEN

Care, Don't Control

*"There is nothing harder than the
softness of indifference."*
– Clare Boothe Luce (1903-1987), American playwright,
journalist, congresswoman and diplomat

THE ACC MODEL OF ACCOUNTABILITY	
"WANT-TO"	"HAVE-TO"
Accountable	Not Accountable
APPROACH	ATTACK
CARE	CONTROL
CLARIFY	CONFUSE

When I think about the difference between caring versus
controlling, sometimes the military comes to mind. A
militaristic style is primarily one of control. In the military,
you learn to follow orders. Your commanders dictate many
aspects of your life, including such personal things as when
you eat, what you eat, when you go to sleep and what time
you wake up. When you join the military, that's all part of
the package. You know what to expect when you sign on.

Military training is conducted in that manner to create discipline and a respect for authority; in part, so that on the battlefield, you will do what you're told to do without hesitation. In battle, there's no time for negotiation. You can't say, "Gee, Lieutenant Peters, I've got a better idea." You can't say, "Well, I've got a cold, and I really don't feel like going out in this rainy weather today."

> **When leaders treat every problem as if it's a crisis, and treat their employees like soldiers, those employees eventually get "combat fatigue" and burn out.**

The military's command and control style is highly effective. Soldiers risk their lives in service to our country. We owe a debt of gratitude to all the men and women serving in our Armed Forces.

I'm proud to say that I served in the Air Force for about four years right after high school. Looking back, I can see how the experience shaped me. Though difficult at times, I found it very instructive. I learned that the command-and-control style has its place. I learned first-hand that there are times—as in war—that leaders must take charge.

Some workplace situations require this style as well: in a desperate turnaround situation, for example, when a company is fighting for its life.

It's also necessary during lunchtime at a busy restaurant. Waiters need to deliver hot food to the tables fast; they don't have time to offer the chef advice about the menu. A manager will say, "Take this to Table 18." Period.

An emergency room is another obvious example. The physicians, nurses, and technicians don't have time to engage in long extraneous conversations. No one will ask how others feel about their work, or their lives. The physicians will call the shots and everyone else will obey. Period.

The problem arises when the command style is used in an ordinary corporate setting. When leaders treat every problem as if it's a crisis, and treat their employees like soldiers, those employees eventually get "combat fatigue" and burn out.

Here are the three primary problems with the control style in the business setting.

Controlling Managers Don't Capitalize on Employees' Strengths

Let's consider the example of Beth. Beth was the CEO of a distribution company that had been experiencing high turnover among its managers. This issue prompted Beth to engage me to help her become a more effective leader and improve her relationships with her employees. Beth also was concerned with creating more balance between her work and personal life. I had been working with Beth for a short time when she asked me to "shadow" her for a day.

Shadow coaching is a way for leaders to obtain detailed feedback on their personal leadership style. It creates more self awareness and an ability to recognize effective and ineffective behaviors. With that information, leaders can make a choice about what they want, while being fully aware of what they actually are doing.

When I'm shadow coaching a client, I spend time at the client's place of business observing him or her on a typical day. I note the client's behaviors, habits and interactions with others. I sit in on meetings to see how the client facilitates group discussions. I observe a coaching session with one of the client's employees. Sometimes I even watch how the client handles daily routines such as scheduling, paperwork, emails and phone calls. Later, we debrief, and I share what I've observed.

The day of Beth's shadow coaching, we began by spending some time in her office. Although her desk was clear, there were piles of paperwork stacked on the floor all around the room. She spent considerable time searching for a report she wanted to discuss with me. She was frequently interrupted by staff members coming in to her office with quick updates.

I asked Beth whether any of the projects she was working on could be delegated to someone else in order to free up some of her time. "Yeah, I wish I could," Beth said. "But everybody's too busy to take on anything else right now. That's something I need your help with. I'm working way too many hours."

I thought about that for a minute. "Let's start with something basic," I said. "What's one small project you could assign to one of your managers?"

"Oh, I really can't think of anything," Beth replied. "I tried that once with my purchasing manager, and he ended up messing up a big order with one of our major suppliers."

"Okay," I said. "We can revisit that later. What about your assistant? What could she help with?"

"Nothing, really. I'm afraid she's got all that she can handle," Beth said. "Plus, she's not up to speed with our software program, so I have to run all the management reports myself."

Later that day, I observed a coaching session Beth conducted with Wayne, the company's VP of Sales. Both Beth and Wayne were concerned about a recent decline in new customer orders and had agreed to address the problem together.

When Wayne arrived at Beth's office for the meeting, she got things off to a good start by coming out from behind her desk and inviting Wayne to be seated at a small conference table. Although it wasn't ideal to hold the meeting there (her office, her turf), Beth evened the playing field a bit with the seating arrangement.

As the coaching session began, Beth seemed a bit self-conscious about having me present. However, it didn't take long before Beth and Wayne both seemed to forget that I was in the room.

Wayne began, "As you already know, the sales guys are doing a great job with our current customers. However, they're not meeting our goals for opening new accounts so far this year. I know it's only May, but I'm a little concerned about it and I wanted to get your take on what's going on."

Following proper coaching technique, Beth asked, "What do you think is contributing to the problem, Wayne?"

"Well, from what I can gather, we're definitely getting up to bat. They're getting the appointments. But they're not getting the sales. I've gone on a few calls with them lately and it seems like maybe some of our newer reps aren't as familiar with our product lines as they should be. They're not able to field some of the more technical questions that prospects are asking."

Beth was taking notes and nodding as Wayne explained how he saw the problem.

"So you think our sales reps need more training," Beth said. "You know, we've already spent a considerable amount of time and money on training these guys."

"Well, uh …" Wayne hesitated. "I know we gave them *some* training…"

"So if they've already been trained, then what's the real problem?" Beth interrupted. Though she continued to take notes and maintain eye contact, Beth inched forward in her chair, leaning her elbows onto the conference table.

"I'm just saying that I think we need more *focused* training," Wayne replied defensively. "Not just in our product lines, Beth, but in preparing for sales calls and maybe even something on relationship selling. You know, you wanted to hire people with minimal sales experience, and I understood your point about wanting to teach them our way of doing things. But the problem is, we're not really giving them the support they need."

"Well, I have to disagree with you there, Wayne. But let's just say we do it your way. How is that going to help us meet our goals this month or next?"

"You know what I think?" Beth continued before he could answer. "I think you need to take a more active role in these sales calls. You know our product line almost as well as I do. So I really think you should be going out with the new guys to make sure they don't lose any more sales. I think you understand, Wayne, we just can't afford for this situation to continue."

"Wait a minute," Wayne said. "I think you've misunderstood. Training isn't the only issue that's contributing to the problem. I wanted to talk to you about our shipping schedules and our return policy…"

But before Wayne could finish, Beth cut the meeting short. "Look, Wayne. I know you're stressed out that your team isn't hitting its goals. I mean, it affects all of us when the sales aren't there and you must be feeling bad about that. So I suggest that you go back to your office and take a look at your travel schedule. You'll feel a whole lot better if you just step things up and make sure we close some new accounts—the sooner the better."

After the meeting, we returned to Beth's office. "Poor guy," she began, "sometimes he just isn't able to get to the root of things. I guess you picked up on that, Alan."

"Yes, it was an interesting meeting. I was able to pick up on several things," I responded neutrally. "How do *you* think the meeting went, Beth?"

"I thought it was pretty good, actually. I'm glad I was able to help Wayne get clear on what he needed to do. He's got some great ideas, but he just needs help moving things to action."

"Great. I saw you took some notes during the meeting. What were some of the ideas Wayne came up with that you wrote down?"

As Beth examined her notes, she realized that she had not captured and could not recall much of what Wayne had contributed.

"Well, Wayne started off by talking about what he sees as a training problem, so we just went right there," Beth explained. "You know, I try not to let my employees indulge in too many excuses. I think that's an important part of being a coach-manager, don't you, Alan?"

"Yes, I do, Beth. And there are some other aspects of being a coach-manager that you asked me to observe and provide feedback on. May I share some of my observations with you?"

With Beth's permission, I let her know that she had unconsciously controlled the discussion with Wayne and had therefore, controlled the outcome of the coaching session.

"Beth, you hired Wayne for his sales management skills and experience. He sees first-hand the challenges faced by his sales team. Yet you didn't really give Wayne an opportunity to explain what was going on, or how he might address the problems. From my vantage point, it would be worth your time to listen to all of Wayne's ideas, and coach him through any difficulties he's experiencing. That means doing a lot more asking than telling. What do you think, Beth?"

Beth conceded that she shouldn't have tried to do Wayne's job for him. She acknowledged that she needed to do a better job of listening, and tapping into Wayne's knowledge and expertise. And Beth learned, over time, that her effectiveness as a leader would come from working through people, rather than trying to control them.

Let me ask you a question. Have you ever attended a meeting like the one between Wayne and Beth? I bet you have.

Now here's a tougher question: Have you have ever *conducted* a meeting like that? If so, you're not alone.

Like Beth, many leaders are confident, dynamic and intelligent people. They know a lot. They're busy. They're aware of the issues and they're eager to tell their people how to fix the problems. Even leaders and managers with the best of intentions can inadvertently control a meeting and make employees feel intimidated, reluctant to speak up or to regret doing so. Unfortunately, their desire to control does not capitalize on their employees' strengths. It just makes them more dependent. In essence, controlling behavior wastes company resources.

Controlling Managers Don't Develop Talent for the Future

Let's assume for a moment that you can actually have a good relationship with your employees while using a controlling style. For argument's sake, let's say that they don't rebel, they don't ignore you, and they don't resign. Still, what will you have a year from now, or two years from now? You'll have the same staff you have right now. They'll have the exact same skills and abilities—no better. When you control people, you inhibit—even *prohibit*—their growth and development.

Think about Wayne. As he sat there silently and glumly at the conference table, was he engaged in creative, productive, stimulated thinking? Was he learning?

> **No one wishes his or her boss were *more* controlling.**

No. Once Wayne realized that Beth was not really listening to anything he said, his openness to her ideas and comments disappeared. Instead, he just became resentful of Beth's communication and leadership style.

Controlling Managers Contribute to High Turnover

Naturally, talented people want to use their talents. Naturally, intelligent people want to use their brains. Therefore, controlling managers fail to attract and retain the most talented people.

"Oh, he's so controlling!" is one of the most common complaints employees make about their managers. That's never a compliment. No one wishes his or her boss were *more* controlling.

People control in various ways. They don't always rant and rave. They're not always openly abusive or angry. In fact, whispers can be quite controlling as well, if they exclude other people.

The best way to recognize controlling behavior is by your own response to it.

Are you asked for your opinions? If not, how do you feel about that?

Are your opinions taken seriously? If not, how do you feel about that?

When you're speaking, is your supervisor just pretending to listen, while actually preparing his or her next remarks? If so, how do you feel about that?

When meeting with your supervisor, does he or she do all the talking? Often that's the best clue: one-way communication. If you're told what to do—or telling others what to do—chances are you're in a controlling, and ineffective environment. And chances are, high turnover will result.

The Caring Solution

What's the opposite of command and control leadership? Caring.

Stay with me. This is not "touchy-feely." It's simple human caring, and it's something all employees need if they're going to achieve the goals you want them to achieve.

A leader from the sports world comes to mind. Phil Jackson, one of the most successful basketball coaches ever, gives his players books to read—a different book chosen specifically for each player. He shares his spiritual perspective, shaped by his study of Zen and Native American traditions. He rarely raises his voice.

Most strikingly, he listens to his players, asking for their input, even during games. The NBA's career leader in playoff victories and playoff winning percentage, Jackson has won nine NBA titles, tying Red Auerbach for the most ever. In other words, he's one of the very best coaches.

What's his main message to his players? "I care about you as people."

Here's the most compelling thing about caring: it works.

In a *Fast Company* article in September 2005 ("The CEO's New Clothes"), Linda Tischler maintains that Morgan Stanley's Philip Purcell, Hewlett-Packard's Carly Fiorina, and Disney's Michael Eisner all lost their jobs because their management styles tripped them up. But not because of the ostensible reasons of "failed strategies, shareholder lawsuits, and missed earnings."

"Purcell was an autocrat who treated his own employees with contempt," the article says. "Eisner was smart and creative, but also paranoid and unwilling to share power." Fiorina, the article continues, was the "queen of the keynote" but was "so inept at minding business back at the mothership, that her successor, the consummately hands-on Mark Hurd, is being heralded as the 'anti-Carly.'"

Tischler goes on to note that domination is no longer in fashion. "Imperiousness is so five minutes ago. Autumn's hot look for bosses is the ability to rally the troops behind the organization's mission and objectives. Heard of it? It's called leadership. Boards are increasingly looking for CEOs who can demonstrate superb people skills in dealing with employees or other stakeholders while delivering consistent results."

What exactly are people skills? Attitudes like respect and acceptance. Activities like listening. Asking questions because you care, and because you respect the people who report to you. Easy joking. Camaraderie. In other words—caring.

Tischler's *Fast Company* article also referenced the "Firms of Endearment" study recently completed by Raj Sisodia, professor of marketing at Bentley College, Jag Sheth of Emory University, and writer David Wolfe, which sought a correlation between people skills and profits. They began their research with several hundred top firms and examined such measures as: How did each company treat their suppliers, the environment, and their communities? How successful were their CEOs at inspiring employees?

After completing detailed case studies on 60 of these firms, they came up with a list of 35 companies that had the best records. In looking at financial performance, the researchers found that the "firms of endearment" companies (among them, Whole Foods, Costco, Toyota, Best Buy and JetBlue) returned 758 percent over a recent 10 year period, versus 128 percent for the S&P 500. In each case, the researchers reported that the "firms of endearment" companies were led by "CEOs who inspire respect, loyalty, and even affection, rather than fear."

Think about your own situation. Does your boss inspire fear or respect? Does he or she seem to care about you as a person? Do you truly care about *your* employees?

When you care about your employees, you hold them accountable with love. What is "accountability with love"? It's being tough-minded and open-hearted at the same time. It's caring about who your employees are as people. It's about supporting them as people. It's about appreciating their strengths, their good will, and their desire to achieve and grow and produce.

But *love*? Am I really telling you to *love* your employees? Well, yes. I am.

What if you don't even like them? It may seem esoteric, but try this and see what happens. When you look for the good in people, and open your heart to them, your feelings may change. When you commit to loving them, even if you don't like them, you may find yourself genuinely feeling more compassionate and more appreciative.

Of course, your kindness may also change them, and change your relationship with them. Love is to people what water is to plants. Love makes people grow, and it makes them healthier. Therefore, even if you don't

Kindness works. Caring pays off. Love becomes profitable.

like someone, if you make an attempt to love them, that attempt is likely to change you, that other person, and your relationship.

Which of course, is good for business. Kindness works. Caring pays off. Love becomes profitable.

It feels better, too; to your employees, but also to you. You don't really want the people you supervise to fear you, do you? You don't really want them to go home unhappy, do you? Resenting you and your management style? Wouldn't it be more satisfying if they liked you, admired you, if they went home at night and exclaimed, "I'm so lucky to have the supervisor I have!" That's what a little caring can do for them—and for you.

CHAPTER ELEVEN

Clarify, Don't Confuse

*"I have found that being honest is
the best technique I can use.*
– Lee Iacocca, former chairman of
the Chrysler Corporation

THE ACC MODEL OF ACCOUNTABILITY	
"WANT-TO"	"HAVE-TO"
Accountable	Not Accountable
APPROACH	ATTACK
CARE	CONTROL
CLARIFY	CONFUSE

This is a story about the four people named
Everybody, Somebody, Anybody, and *Nobody.*
There was an important job to be done and
Everybody was sure that *Somebody* would do it.
Anybody could have done it, but *Nobody* did it.
Somebody got angry, because it was *Everybody's* job.
Everybody thought *Anybody* could do it, but
Nobody realized that *Everybody* wouldn't do it.
So *Everybody* blamed *Somebody* when
Nobody did what *Anybody* could have done.

– Anonymous

Talk about confusion! How's that for an illustration of how miscommunication can lead to anger, blame, and a lack of accountability?

You already may be a clear communicator. I have no reason to believe that you're not. I do believe, however, that communication is an essential element of accountability, that everyone can become better at communicating, and that The Accountability System tools can help everybody (as well as anybody and somebody) improve.

> **Despite your best intentions, your employees may not understand something as simple as what their job entails.**

Despite their best intentions, managers sometimes make it more difficult for their people to be accountable. Let's consider some of the ways managers may inadvertently confuse their employees, and how that compromises accountability.

Unclear about Overall Roles or Goals

Despite your best intentions, your employees may not understand something as simple as what their job entails. How many of your employees have a job description? How many employees—and managers—take performance reviews seriously? Managers might think employees are clear about their roles and responsibilities, but often, that's simply not the case. And if managers never raise the issue, employees are likely to stay in the dark, fumbling around ineffectively.

In a survey published in *Coaching For Improved Work Performance (McGraw-Hill 2000)*, author Ferdinand F. Fournies asked 4,000 managers: "Why don't employees do what they're supposed to do?"

The response chosen either first or second, 99 percent of the time, was: ***They don't know what they're supposed to do.***

Yet, when managers try to solve individual performance problems, Fournies says, they rarely begin at the beginning: helping people understand exactly what they're supposed to do.

Accountability begins with people really understanding what we expect from them. (You might say it even begins before that: with *our* understanding of what we expect from other people. If we don't know, how can we expect others to know?)

If you're not in the habit of clarifying these things, you're probably confusing your staff.

My clients don't always believe me on that point, and you might not either. But here's an actual example of how this happens.

I recently was talking with Dwayne, the managing director of a large professional services firm, about a problem he had with one of his senior consultants. "Is it possible that Tamara just doesn't know what to do or how to do it?" I asked.

"No way!" he said emphatically. "She's been with me for 12 years."

But those 12 years might be adding to the miscommunication. Sometimes, long-time employees are even *less* likely to understand what's needed, because they dare not ask, and you dare not tell them. Both sides assume that the employee *must* understand what's expected, because he or she has been there "forever." But longevity doesn't necessarily add up to mind reading.

Other clients protest, "What, are you crazy?! He's making $130 grand!" Or, "She's got an MBA!" Of course, these people know what to do... or do they?

I guarantee you that a high salary alone does not ensure that people understand what you want them to do. Nor do advanced degrees. And like longevity, these factors can actually interfere with your communication. If you assume that people *should* know, and *should not* require your time or attention, you're more likely to overlook their need for instruction and guidance.

> **No matter how successful, educated, or highly compensated people are, they won't "automatically" be clear about their responsibilities.**

No matter how successful, educated, or highly compensated people are, they won't "automatically" be clear about their responsibilities. If you're supervising them, it's your job to make sure they know what to do, and how. The only way to do that is through clear communication.

Unclear about Task Expectations

Another thing that contributes to confusion is when people are not clear about what you expect from them on a particular task. As new assignments are made, managers are not always clear about what they expect of people that day, or that week, or for that project. They're too busy to stop, so they make quick assignments, often communicating these assignments in the hallway, without even really making eye contact. Then they're surprised later when the results are not acceptable.

Consider for a moment: What exactly do you expect from each of your employees regarding particular projects?

How often do you articulate what that is? Often, managers' expectations are vague, and tinged with exasperation: "I want Paul to write the annual report for the board of directors, obviously!"

But how should it compare to last year's report? What feedback from the board should be incorporated? Why did you choose Paul for this assignment? Which of his strengths do you expect him to draw on in order to accomplish it? What are the standards? The same as last year? Better?

Those every day situations and interactions provide you with an opportunity to build accountability into your culture. Conversely, when you're not clear about outcomes or responsibilities or expectations, it leads to confusion. Throw a lack of feedback into the mix and you've got the makings of what I call "The 50/150 Percent Situation."

The 50/150 Percent Situation

Some years ago, I had the pleasure of working with an executive on the West Coast that I'll call Jamie. Jamie had been working in manufacturing for years, and had worked his way up the corporate ladder to plant manager in a sizeable, profitable company.

When that company was sold to a larger manufacturer, Jamie stayed on and became the chief operating officer. Then *that* company merged with an even larger manufacturer, and in the space of just three years, Jamie moved from being a plant manager in a $60 million dollar company to being the president of a $250 million dollar division of a $5 billion dollar international conglomerate.

In the months following the merger, Jamie had his hands full acclimating to the new environment and a much larger scope of authority. He now had a total workforce of 1,200 people and eight senior managers reporting to him, most of whom had been with the international company for years prior to the merger.

Being the "new kid on the block," Jamie wasn't inclined to make a lot of changes right away. Thankfully, he thought, *my senior managers all have been here for awhile, and they know the ropes.*

But six months into the job, Jamie's division was experiencing some real quality issues. Scrap and rework costs had gone up. Cycle times were off the mark. Customer delivery dates were running late.

At first, Jamie just chalked it up to the normal growing pains of the merger. And certainly, that contributed to the problem. But over the next few weeks, as he started digging into the problems, he found evidence of poor performance among his senior managers. So he called them all into the boardroom for a meeting, and proceeded to rake them over the coals.

"What in the world have you all been doing the last six months?! The quality around here stinks and you don't seem to give two hoots about on-time delivery! I'd like to know just which one of you is going to take responsibility for getting quality under control! Do you have any idea how much these customer returns are costing us?! You're not doing *this*, you need to do more of *that*..." and on and on he went.

Needless to say, Jamie's eight managers were stunned. Who was this guy? Where did he get off telling them how to do their jobs? They were already working themselves to the bone—what more did he want?

Later, when Jamie and I discussed this in an accountability coaching session, he came to realize that his behavior at that meeting had widened a gap that already existed between him and his senior managers. A gap that had first been created when Jamie chose to let his inherited employees go their own way because "they knew the ropes."

In the absence of real, meaningful interaction and feedback from Jamie, those managers thought they were doing just fine: "No news is good news, so everything must be hunky-dory." They thought they were performing at 100 percent.

But Jamie, now *he's* thinking something completely different. He's thinking his managers are performing at maybe 50 percent. And so he calls them into the boardroom and delivers the "one-two punch." And his managers walk away thinking, "Boy, I was already doing 100 percent, but he's certainly not happy with that! I guess I've got to work at 150 percent!"

Instead of closing the performance gap with his managers, Jamie widened it. He made his job so much harder than it needed to be. What Jamie realized too late was that had he been clear from the very beginning about what he expected, he could have avoided the 50/150 Percent Situation.

PART THREE

The Coach Approach:

Implementing The Accountability System

CHAPTER TWELVE

Job Description of a Coach-Manager

"I never cease to be amazed at the power
of the coaching process to draw out the skills
or talent that was previously hidden within an
individual, and which invariably finds a way to
solve a problem previously thought unsolvable."
– John Russell, vice president, Harley-Davidson Europe

You have now arrived at the "how" part of the book. This is where you'll learn the tools, tips and techniques that will assist you in taking The Accountability System from interesting theory to effective practice. What matters from now on is not just how well you understand The Accountability System, but also how well you implement it.

I've filled this section of the book with everything I can think of to help you be successful. But you don't have to do it all, and you don't even have to do it well—not at first, when you're just getting your feet wet. Every situation is unique, so use the tools that make the most sense to you.

Fundamental to The Accountability System is your willingness to claim the role of coach-manager and to meet with your employees in regularly scheduled accountability coaching sessions. I'll talk more about that in the next chapter, but to give you a glimpse of what's possible, let me tell you about my client Brian.

> **Fundamental to The Accountability System is your willingness to claim the role of coach-manager and to meet with your employees in regularly scheduled accountability coaching sessions.**

Brian is in the residential real estate business. During one of our coaching sessions, Brian mentioned that he had some unsold properties "in the drawer," as he called it.

"How many unsold properties are you sitting on?" I asked.

"Three," he said.

"And how much are they worth to you?" I asked.

"You mean, how much money would I make if I sold them?"

"Yes. How much would you personally profit?"

"I guess I'd make about $220,000 altogether," he said. "I just need to make a few repairs and get them on the market. I think they'd sell pretty quickly."

My eyebrows jumped. "So what you're saying is that you've got $220,000 sitting in your desk drawer, and you're not doing anything about it?"

"Well, uh, I guess you could look at it that way."

I did. So I paused, waiting for Brian to see what I saw. He didn't comment, and didn't seem motivated to take any particular action.

"Let me send you my address," I said. "Since you're not very interested in that $220,000, go ahead and send it to me. I can think of a few things to do with it."

Finally, Brian laughed. Together, we devised an action plan that would help him take the steps necessary to convert that "drawer money" into real money.

The sales didn't happen overnight. We met in regularly scheduled coaching sessions to review his plans, assess the factors that continued to block his progress, remove the barriers, and achieve results. Because we had a clear understanding about our relationship and expectations, I was able to continue gently challenging Brian until he sold all three properties.

When the final sale was complete, Brian decided to celebrate in a big way. He and his wife took the Alaskan cruise they'd been dreaming of for years.

I can't take any credit for Brian's profitable deals. This is an accountability coaching success story, and I share it as a way to remind you of what your employees could be achieving, once you learn how to hold them accountable. They, too, have "drawer money" that they're not converting to cash, new customers, new ideas, or whatever their responsibilities entail. But they haven't done it yet because they're distracted, stuck, don't know what to do, or are otherwise unable to achieve certain things without some coaching.

That's okay. That's where you come in. They need you. With your willingness, their willingness, plus a few coaching tools, you can cash in together. It all begins with stepping up to the plate and saying "yes" to becoming a coach-manager. Before I define that, let me give you a little background on coaching, because it puts the coach-manager role into context.

What Is a Coach?

The word coach doesn't mean what it used to. Coach used to refer to my baseball mentor Mr. G., or Mrs. Walker, the physical education teacher who coached the girls' field hockey team, or all those neighborhood Moms and Dads who taught us how to compete, keep score, swim, shoot hoops, throw spirals, and catch fly balls.

Nowadays, there are still sports coaches, of course, but the word "coach" also refers to a trained business professional who helps other businesspeople stay on track. Everywhere you go, it seems, you meet consultants who call themselves coaches. There are life coaches, career coaches, transition coaches, strategy coaches, performance coaches, success coaches, public speaking coaches, and lots more. Some are certified, some are not. Some are qualified, some are not. In the United States, coaching has become a billion dollar a year industry.

To gain some control over this burgeoning field, the Lexington, Kentucky-based International Coach Federation—which now boasts more than 10,000 members and more than 132 chapters in 34 countries—certifies coaches based on their training and experience, and establishes ethical standards, including client confidentiality. Coach U, one of the largest coach-training organizations, offers classes, seminars, and conferences, as do some universities, such as Georgetown University.

That's the route I took. After many years as a business owner, I went back to school, graduated from Coach U, and joined the International Coach Federation, as well as other related professional associations. I now specialize in leadership development for business owners, CEOs, executives and their teams. I use my coaching skills and business experience to help clients make improvements with people, productivity and profitability.

Because I spend a lot of time in-
side companies, people sometimes
refer to what I do as training. My
work includes some training, but it's
mostly coaching, and I think that's
an important distinction. Training is
an event. Coaching is *a process that
takes place over time.*

> **Coaches are advisors, mentors, leaders, listeners, facilitators, confidants, and guides.**

In *Spin Selling*, author Neil Rackham notes that almost all training is ineffective without follow-up coaching. "How-ever excellent your classroom training," he writes, "without good coaching, you are probably wasting 87 cents out of every skills dollar you spend."

All that useful information, going by the wayside! Em-ployees notice this, and some have become cynical about it: "Oh no, not another rah-rah, sis-boom-bah training program that we'll forget about next week!"

Coaching, in contrast, is sustainable. The old Chinese prov-erb comes to mind: "Give a man a fish, and you feed him for a day. Teach a man to fish, and you feed him for a lifetime."

Coaching is about teaching people to fish. When I coach people, I offer them tools they can use for the rest of their lives, in and beyond the workplace. That's what I want you to do with your employees: teach them how to fish.

Teaching is a significant part of coaching. But coaching is also more than that. Coaches are advisors, mentors, lead-ers, listeners, facilitators, confidants, and guides.

There are almost as many definitions of coaching as there are coaches! Here are some of the definitions that might resonate with you:

1. Provide a supportive framework in which people are challenged and encouraged to reach their full potential.

2. Use observation and effective listening skills to help people clearly understand their current situation.

3. Help people tap into their own creativity and re-sourcefulness to uncover strategies that will help them achieve their goals.

4. Provide focus, clarity and awareness of possibilities that will lead to effective choices.

5. Empower people to achieve tangible, sustainable results in productivity, relationships, satisfaction with life and work and the achievement of personal and professional goals.

The coaching process inevitably includes listening, supporting, encouraging, teaching, developing, challenging and more. But essentially, a coach is a guide. Exactly how much progress is made as a result of the coaching relationship is largely up to the person being coached.

As I said, I don't give myself credit for the changes my clients are able to make. I do give credit to the coaching process, however, and to coaching tools. That's why much of my business life is now devoted to teaching managers how to become coach-managers. No matter how many business coaches there may be (and, yes, there are a lot of us!) there can never be enough for every working person.

Yet every working person has a supervisor. And if all, or even a lot, of those supervisors learned to become coach-managers, the workplace would be a very different sort of environment.

What Then, Is a Coach-Manager?

A coach-manager is a manager or leader who consistently uses coaching principles and techniques to improve performance, relationships, and morale.

In other words, a coach-manager is someone who ensures accountability in the workplace, using a coach-like approach.

Because coaching has become so popular, many managers use coaching jargon or have adopted some coaching techniques. "I coach all the time," managers tell me. "Why do I need to formalize it?"

Note that my definition includes the word <u>consistently</u>. If you're not consistently using the principles and techniques, you're not really coaching—any more than the Mom or Dad who plays catch with Michael or Megan in the backyard is really coaching.

A Coach-Manager DOES	A Coach-Manager Does NOT
Ask and listen	Tell and lecture
Focus on the employee's agenda	Focus on his or her own agenda
Say: "Tell me how I can help"	Say: "Here's what I need you to do"
Help employees solve and prevent problems	Solve the employees' problems for them
Model leadership behavior for employees	Tell employees how they should act
Help employees hold themselves accountable for progress and results	Accept fault, blame or excuses

You may wonder: Isn't coach-managing the same as managing? Well, you tell me. Do most managers *consistently use coaching principles and techniques to improve performance, relationships, and morale?*

No. That's why I distinguish between a manager and a coach-manager. I'm asking you to add coaching to your work role, and even to your identity.

Here's the most significant difference between a regular manager/employee relationship and a coach-manager/employee relationship: *the focus is on the person being coached, rather than on the work alone.* You keep the task in mind, of course; you're both there to achieve business results. But as a coach-manager, many of your interactions are about—and for—the employee.

Instead of focusing only on the task—"When will the ABC project be completed?"—the coach-manager also focuses on the person: "How are you doing with the ABC project? What sort of resources do you need? How can I support you?"

> **The person being coached gains a great deal of autonomy, *and thus, feels more accountable for the outcome of the work.***

Do you see the difference? Can you imagine how it feels to hear a question about a project, versus a question about you?

This is a big change for many managers. They protest: "I don't have time to ask how people are doing, I just need them to get things done!"

I understand. Coaching does take time. But so does complaining about poor performance. So does taking on tasks yourself because your people aren't following through. So does firing people, and looking for new people to hire.

Ironically, when a manager becomes a coach-manager, the employee becomes "the boss" in some ways. The employee sets the agenda for many meetings. The employee has a great deal of input on the goals to achieve. Those goals must be in alignment with the organization's goals, of course, but they're the employee's goals nevertheless. The employee feels an ownership, and a sense of responsibility. As the employee encounters problems, he or she is asked to solve them—with support and guidance from the manager, and with respect, encouragement and faith in the employee's problem-solving ability. All of this, as you might imagine, helps boost the employee's confidence and builds skills for the future.

Here's another hidden benefit. Even though the coach-manager and employee will meet more often than they probably did in the past, the employee being coached gains a great deal of autonomy, *and thus, feels more accountable for the outcome of the work.*

Adjusting to the coach-manager role can be challenging. There are times when you need to lead and direct, and there are times when you need to focus on developing and growing your people. It can take time to integrate wearing the two different hats. Ideally, the coach-manager role will become integrated for you, so that you'll find a way to keep both interests at heart—yours and the employee's—at all times.

And what if you make mistakes? You will. First, forgive yourself. Then, make sure you're creating a climate in which your employees know they can and will make mistakes, too.

In the game of golf, there is a phenomenon called a "mulligan." If you play golf, you've probably given mulligans to yourself, or other players. Mulligans are gifts. Usually, they're given after a mistake, such as a poor shot.

It's a chance to start over without penalty. The gift is, "Go ahead and try again. We won't count that stroke against your score." The mulligan is a second chance; a form of forgiveness; a way to let someone start anew, without penalty.

Mulligans also can be gifts upfront, before you've even taken a swing. Some groups decide to give a mulligan on the first hole. That way, you know that if you don't get off to a good start, you can have a second chance.

I find this to be a useful concept in coaching, and in my personal relationships. Here's how this can work for you. First, explain the mulligan concept to your employee, significant other, child, business partner, associate, co-worker or team. Next, use mulligans in your conversations. If you say something unintentionally hurtful, ask for a mulligan, then try again in a more pleasant, less blaming (and more effective) manner. Mulligans can lighten things up, can remind both of you of your fundamental culture of caring, and can allow you to start anew.

What's the Difference between Empowering and Enabling?

As a coach-manager, your job is to help each team member take personal responsibility for his or her behaviors, actions and results. Your responsibility is to guide and assist them in working toward their professional goals, and to eliminate the barriers to achieving those goals. You're there to empower them. You're not there to do it *for* them.

The essence of coaching is empowerment. To *empower* is to give people power and authority, or remind them of their power and authority.

To *enable* is traditionally defined as "to provide someone with the resources, authority, or opportunity to do something;

to make something possible or feasible." At first glance, it sounds a lot like being a coach-manager, doesn't it?

But the word *enable* is sometimes used in an inverted sense: to enable a person to do something that is not ultimately in their best interest. You may have heard the word used this way in relation to alcoholism. Spouses are encouraged not to "enable" their alcoholic loved ones by, for instance, calling in sick for them, or otherwise enabling them to keep drinking excessively. In this context, becoming an "enabler" is not something you want to do.

Some managers enable people to remain dependent or lackadaisical. If, for instance, an employee handles a project poorly, and you re-do it yourself, you're enabling your employee to remain unskilled. Instead of empowering them to grow, learn, or develop, you've done their work for them, and thus actually hindered their progress.

> "Every morning, when I get to work, there's a line at my door."

Here's an example of enabling. The owner of a large electronics business (let's call him Joe) engaged me, and in our first coaching session, he complained, "I'm working way too many hours."

Of course, I said, "Tell me more about that."

"Well, every day at 5:00 or 5:30 in the evening," he said, "all my employees are walking by my office, waving goodbye to go home, and I'm stuck here until 8:30 or 9:00 at night. This is really getting old."

As we talked about that, and I asked open-ended questions to uncover what was taking up so much time, Joe explained, "Every morning, when I get to work, there's a line outside my door."

"What do you mean?" I asked.

"My managers are lined up, waiting to come in to talk to me," he said.

"Why?" I asked.

"They need to know what to do."

"Then what happens?"

"I tell them what to do!"

"Okay, what happens then?"

"Then the next day, we're right back to where we started. Another line outside my door."

As you've already gathered, Joe was enabling his employees to remain dependent on him for all the answers. No wonder they kept lining up at his door. They didn't have to think for themselves. They didn't have to worry about being wrong or taking risks. They didn't have to worry about displeasing their boss. They didn't have to be accountable for their actions. They just asked him what to do, and he told them. Easy!

But they were stagnating, and Joe was exhausted.

So of course I reminded him of the fish story. Joe was standing in his office, handing out fish every day, instead of developing his people.

Here's a domestic example. If you're a parent, and your six-year-old leaves her socks on the floor every day, and you pick them up, what's going to happen? Of course, she's going to keep dropping her socks on the floor. As long as you tolerate it, and even "enable" it by cleaning up after her, the behavior will continue to happen. The same is true for any behavior, at work or at home.

Sometimes, the managers who have the most trouble learning to empower, rather than enable, are those with high standards. Many readers of this book probably fall into that category. You want things to go well, and you know exactly how to do it, so… it seems easier to just do it yourself. But, of course, you know deep down that this is not in your best interest, nor in the best interest of your employees.

Here are some principles to keep in mind as you practice empowering your employees:

- *Be willing to invest time in delegating and helping your employees do it right.* A little investment now will reap big returns later. No time? Then don't delegate. But keep in mind, if you don't have time now, chances are you won't have time later.

- *Be clear about the results you want to achieve.* Delegate the objective, not the procedure. Your employee may find a more efficient way to get the job done. Don't miss that opportunity by over-managing.

- *Employees need and want new challenges and responsibilities.* These help them to develop professionally, and increase the likelihood that they'll stay with your company as they continue to grow.

- *If the people working for you are not living up to their potential, it's a waste of human resources.* Most of us are conscious of not wasting oil, water, food, paper, and other natural resources. Wasting human resources is just as harmful.

- *As a leader, you need to perform at your highest level.* You can't perform at your highest level if you remain mired in duties that rightfully should be done by others. And if you're not fulfilling your potential, then *you're* wasting the company's resources, too.

Now that you begin to see all that's involved in coaching, why should you bother learning how to become a coach-manager? I'll remind you of the five promises of The Accountability System: improved morale, increased productivity, fewer disciplinary problems, more meaningful performance reviews, and enhanced relationships.

All that can be yours when you become a coach-manager. Accountability will become an integral part of your workplace, as ordinary and expected as lunchtime and payday.

Chapter Thirteen

Regularly Scheduled Accountability Coaching

"There will be two buses leaving
the hotel for the park tomorrow.
The two o'clock bus will be for those
of you who need a little extra work.
The empty bus will leave at five o'clock."
– Dave Bristol, former Major League Baseball manager

Earlier, you learned that in order to have accountability, you need three things: a culture, a process, and you.

To have accountability, you must first be willing to take responsibility for yourself and the performance of your people. The buck starts here—with you.

To have accountability, you also must create a culture in which approaching, caring and clarifying are evident in all you do. A culture in which employees want to be there, want to perform, and want to succeed.

And to have accountability, you need a process: a means of working with and through your employees on a regular basis, guiding them toward their best possible achievements.

That process is through regularly scheduled accountability coaching sessions. This is where your role as an accountability coach-manager really comes in. When you begin meeting with your people on a regular basis, your relationship with them will improve, their performance will improve, and your mutual results will improve. Accountability will become the norm, and not the exception.

What Is an Accountability Coaching Session?

A coaching session is not a lecture. It's not a scolding, speech, or reprimand. It's not a boss telling a subordinate what to do. It's not a performance review meeting, and it's not a business meeting.

A coaching session is a conversation. It's an exchange of ideas, plans, feelings, hopes, and dreams. But it's more than that—it's about getting into action. A coaching session's two-way dialogue leads to the creation of plans that are then reviewed and discussed again in the next coaching session, creating a climate of action and mutual accountability.

As a coach-manager, your job is to support employees in achieving their goals, not to do it for them. So a large part of coaching sessions is helping employees to discover creative solutions to problems. There will be times when you'll be tempted to just tell them what to do. That would make things so much easier, wouldn't it? Not in the long run. As we've already seen, that would create a "line outside your door," and a situation in which your employees are dependent on you to tell them what to do.

Most important to remember: Accountability coaching sessions are about *them*, not about *you*.

Why Regularly Scheduled?

Perhaps some of you, like me, are frequent business travelers. Whenever I board a plane, I'm always tempted to peek into the cockpit to see what the pilots are doing. On some basic level, I feel comforted when I spot the captain holding a piece of paper, pen in hand, studying what I imagine is a preflight checklist. As I board my flight, I'm assuming, of course, that the pilot already knows how to fly the plane. But seeing that checklist lets me know that the pilot's objectives are the same as mine: making sure we have a safe flight.

As a coach-manager, the best way for you to maintain flight readiness is through regularly scheduled accountability coaching sessions. Note that I didn't say, "casual, periodic, as-needed coaching sessions." I mean, what would happen if pilots ran through the preflight checklist only when they felt like it or had some extra time?

Pilots *always* complete a preflight checklist. No matter how many hours they've flown, no matter how many times they've been in that same plane and found everything to be in order, they go through their preflight routine. They check out the weather, the maintenance log, their instruments, the flight pattern, and dozens of other things, I'm sure.

> **Regular coaching sessions create a climate of action and mutual accountability.**

Now I'm not trying to say that every coaching session involves issues critical to safety. But complacency isn't an option for coach-managers any more than it is for a pilot. To really hold people accountable, you need to be in touch with them routinely and frequently. Regular coaching sessions give you the structure to do that.

Regularly scheduled means at least every other week. *Really? Twice a month?* Yes, really. Once a month is definitely not enough.

First, as a coach-manager, you'll want to capitalize on the learning technique of "spaced repetition." Many studies show that people learn new habits and new material best when they review it in frequent intervals. Otherwise, they forget, or fall back into their old ways.

Second, you'll want to follow up on the goals you discussed and the commitments you made before too much time goes by. If you wait too long, those goals and commitments may have become irrelevant.

> **When meetings are scheduled at regular intervals, your employees will realize very quickly that they can count on you to help them make progress, meet their goals, and get what they want.**

Third, regularly scheduled coaching sessions ultimately will save you time. It's hard to see that at first, when you're adding multiple one-hour sessions to your already crowded calendar. But think about the time you spend cleaning up after staff members who don't do things correctly the first time. Or explaining to your own boss why your team didn't complete a project by deadline. Or doing things that your staff should have handled themselves.

Fourth, and most important to remember: This is not just about you and your need to avoid a crash. When meetings are scheduled at regular intervals, your employees will realize very quickly that they can count on you to help them make progress, meet their goals, and get what they want. Will this make a difference in their performance? Of course it will!

What's the Difference between a Business Meeting and a Coaching Session?

When you add coaching sessions to your schedule, what happens to your business meetings? You still need to meet with your staff as a team, right? And gather in various configurations with other staff members, managers, executives, and customers? Of course. So what's the difference between the two?

Business meetings tend to be in groups. In a business meeting, you identify and discuss problems, celebrate achievements, and plan upcoming actions. You might brainstorm ideas, and you might (and should) specify who's going to do what, and by when. But business meetings tend to be mostly about the transfer of information. People usually

Accountability Coaching IS	Accountability Coaching Is NOT
Regularly scheduled and ongoing	If you get around to it, or if there's a problem
A structured conversation between coach-manager and employee	Informally catching up or getting together just to socialize
Working toward goals and priorities	Working on task lists
Developing the employee's strengths	Managing only for immediate results
Empowering the employee to take better actions	Controlling the employee's actions
Establishing mutual Upfront Agreements	Dictating rules for compliance
The employee saying, "It's my responsibility"	The manager saying "It's your job"

gather, report on progress, ask for input, then disperse and proceed on their own, or with their teams.

Coaching sessions are almost always one-on-one. In a coaching session, you might also identify and discuss problems, celebrate achievements, and plan upcoming actions, but the emphasis is more focused and practical, and at the same time more personal. In a safe, supportive environment, the employee focuses on his or her professional challenges and goals with assistance from a caring, helpful coach-manager.

Together, the two people create action plans that allow the employee to move forward, one step at a time, by committing to specific actions with specific deadlines. All of this happens within the context of individual growth and development.

Where Should Coaching Conversations Take Place?

If at all possible, meet in a neutral location. A conference room is ideal; a coffee shop may be fine from time to time. The point is to get together in a place that's not your office, and not your employee's office, putting the two of you on more equal footing. Be sure to choose a place where you won't be interrupted, where you can have an open, relaxed conversation.

Face-to-face meetings are always best if possible, because they're most conducive to building trust and improving communication. However, if you can't conduct an in-person coaching session, a coaching session by phone is okay, too.

And clearly, many managers supervise employees who do not work in physical proximity to them. You may have employees in another state or even in another country. Perhaps you have employees who telecommute and come in to the office infrequently. It may require more creativity, and you may need some logistical support (teleconference or videoconferencing capabilities, for example), but none of these things has to be a barrier to conducting regular accountability coaching sessions with your employees.

What about Small Talk?

Let's say Juliet shows up for a coaching session on Monday morning. Should you ask her, "How was your weekend? What did you do?" If you ask, you may feel you risk wasting time on social chitchat and distracting from the goals at hand. But if you don't ask, maybe you're failing to establish a caring relationship, and a trusting environment. What to do?

Follow Juliet's lead, but keep your eye on the prize. In other words, if she wants to begin on a social note, fine. If she wants to dive right into the work for the session, let that be fine, too. If, during the preliminaries, she mentions personal issues that may be getting in the way of her work performance, great—you've got an opening to discuss those things. And if, during the opening minutes of the coaching session, she seems to be procrastinating or putting off getting into the coaching discussion, gently guide the session back on track.

Each coaching session will begin very differently, depending on the person you're coaching and "where they are" in that moment. That's good. It demonstrates your flexibility, and your willingness to go with *their* flow.

What Should We Bring to Coaching Sessions?

You and your employee need to bring just two things: your calendar and The Accountability Coaching binder.

Bringing your calendar (whether it's on paper or in an electronic device doesn't matter) ensures that you'll be able to schedule another coaching session before the meeting ends. If you're able to keep to a regular schedule—every Wednesday at 10:00 a.m., for instance—so much the better. You won't have to spend time scheduling. But bring your calendar anyway, just in case you need to change the regular meeting date.

The Accountability Coaching Binder

The Accountability Coaching Binder is a tool that has worked beautifully for my clients in building accountability with their people. It's a three-ring binder in which you will keep important information about an individual employee and the notes from previous coaching sessions with him or her.

Preferably, your binder will have pockets, dividers, and tabs. You can create these binders yourself; you can ask your support staff to do it; or you can ask your coachee to create two binders: one for you, and one for himself or herself. Some people personalize their binders; some put the company logo on it. However you choose to do it, you and your employee should each create or acquire a binder to be used during and between accountability coaching sessions.

Your binder can even have your employee's name on it in big, obvious letters. You might be surprised to learn that it makes a strong impression on employees when you devote a binder specifically to them, and put their name on it. It's a visible symbol that you care about them, are paying attention to them, and are organized in your approach to your work with them.

Some of my clients have tried using one big binder, with tabs separating the material for each of their employees. That usually doesn't work as well as creating separate binders for each of your employees. Separate binders send a strong message about your commitment to them as individuals: You are not just one of my many staff members. You're a separate person, worthy of specific, customized attention. Therefore, if you have four employees, you'll need four binders, one for each person.

Before I describe the contents of The Accountability Coaching Binder, let me address the question some of you are asking: Why paper? Can't we just keep track of things electronically?

I have no particular attachment to paper. If you want to carry a notebook computer to your coaching sessions and record everything there, that's fine. However, many people find the binders easier to carry, easier to refer to together and easier to use for storing a variety of documents. Also, the computer lacks the symbolic value of using a particular item with your staff member's name on it. But whatever works for you is fine. The point is to create an organized place where all relevant documents are accessible, and can easily be supplemented and changed.

Here are some examples of documents that can be stored in each employee's Accountability Coaching Binder:

1) Company mission, vision and values
2) Employee's job description
3) Performance feedback (formal and informal)
4) Goals
5) Individual development plan
6) Upfront Agreement (Chapter 15 is devoted to this subject)
7) Leadership assessments and other professional development resources (360 degree feedback, personality profiles, etc.)

8) Notes from each coaching session

9) "Parking Lot" page or a "revisit" list

10) Blank sheets of paper

What Happens between Coaching Sessions?

Okay, so you've just returned to your office from a coaching session. You begin to review the emails and voice mails that have been waiting for you. You respond to various requests. And before you know it, you've forgotten all about the coaching session. Next thing you know, two weeks have passed, and it's time for another session with you and your employee, Mark. When you and Mark get together, you look at each other blankly. *Where did we leave off? Where should we start? Maybe we should start over? Should we skip these meetings?*

> Use the 48/24 system, and you'll never be caught off guard again, wondering how to jumpstart a coaching session.

Not at all.

This is where the 48/24 tools come in.

Use them, and you'll never be caught off guard again, wondering how to jumpstart an accountability coaching session.

The 48

The "48" refers to the 48 hours immediately following the most recent coaching session. In The Accountability System, Mark will email you a recap of what you discussed within 48 hours. If Mark has taken good notes during the conversation, this will take him no more than about five minutes. (Those who enjoy writing memos may choose to take longer!) The length of the email is immaterial. It's the act of writing it, and sending it to you, the coach-manager, that increases accountability. Whether in long paragraphs or short bullet-points, the 48 email will include these items:

1. Play back:
   - What was discussed and decided, including short-term goals, long-term plans and priorities.
   - Insights and breakthroughs; solutions uncovered; questions that arose and remained unanswered.
   - Anything worth noting from employee to coach-manager.

2. Play forward:
   - What the employee will accomplish between now and the next coaching session.
   - Specific action plans: what, how and by when.

3. Additional questions or concerns that may have emerged after the session.

4. "Parking Lot" items to deal with at a future date.

Feel free to review the sample 48 reports in Appendix B. (These are real reports submitted by employees and coach-managers just like you.)

The 24

The "24" refers to the 24 hours immediately prior to the next coaching session. Within that time period, Mark will email you again. Like the 48, the 24 report has two primary parts:

1. Play back:
   - What was accomplished since the last session, and what was not accomplished?

- If projects were delayed, this part of the note can enumerate some blocks or challenges. (This is not about making excuses; it's a step toward uncovering problems and discussing next steps in the subsequent session.)

2. Play forward:
   - What would the employee like to talk about in the upcoming coaching session?
   - Where is the employee stuck? In what areas does he or she need help? What challenges and opportunities are available now?

In Appendix C, you'll find a sample 24 form that you can use as-is, or modify for your own purposes. Remember, the act of writing things down helps hold people accountable.

Most of my clients use the 48/24 system. It's not essential; it's a choice each coach-manager can make, along with his or her team members. But please note: I'm absolutely, positively convinced that those teams who do use the 48/24 system consistently derive more benefit from the coaching sessions, and are more likely to achieve their desired results. They create more accountability than those teams who do not.

Why is this? When Mark makes a verbal commitment during the coaching session, that's one level of commitment. When he writes it down in The Accountability Binder, that's a second level of commitment. When he types it into an email and sends it to you, that's a third level of commitment. Once Mark has completed all three steps, it's almost impossible for him to say, "Whoops, I forgot." Or, "Whoops, I didn't understand you."

When you begin meeting with your people on a regular basis, the entire team will experience increased activity, productivity, effectiveness and morale. When you make regularly scheduled coaching sessions "just the way we do things around here," accountability is the result.

CHAPTER FOURTEEN

The C.L.E.A.R. Coaching Model

"To teach is to learn twice."

– Joseph Joubert (1754-1824), French essayist and moralist

A t this point, you should have a pretty good understanding of your role as a coach-manager and the importance of regular accountability coaching sessions. You've learned about how coaching sessions differ from business meetings, how frequently they should be conducted, and where they should take place. You've been offered some tips to stay organized and keep records of your progress (in your Accountability Binder) and some tools to guide what takes place between coaching sessions (the 48 and the 24).

> Though all coaching *requires* conversation, not all conversations are *coaching*.

In this chapter, we'll explore a step-by-step process you can use to maximize your effectiveness in each and every coaching session.

Sometimes, my clients refer to accountability coaching sessions as "coaching conversations." That's accurate on the one hand: coaching *does* happen through two-way conversations between an employee and a coach-manager. On the other hand, though all coaching *requires* conversation, not all conversations are *coaching*. (If that were true, then all good conversationalists would necessarily be good coaches, and we know that's not the case.)

The distinction is that in an accountability coaching session, the conversation is intentional, and it's structured.

To be an effective coach-manager, you need a **clear** accountability coaching model to guide the conversation:

- **C** Clarify goals for the coaching session.
- **L** Link back to prior coaching sessions for accountability.
- **E** Explore options and possibilities.
- **A** Accelerate progress by removing barriers.
- **R** Recap the session and confirm commitments.

Let's take a closer look at what happens in each step of the coaching process.

1. Clarify goals for the coaching session – "What's on your mind?"

Let's say you're working with your employee, Debbie. At the beginning of every coaching session, you and Debbie will agree on specific goals, topics and priorities for that session. It may be that you'll pick up on topics you covered the last time you were together. Or it may be that some other issues have come up in the interim that Debbie would like to address. If you're using the 48/24 technique, you'll have a quick reference to the last coaching session and some thoughts on what to cover in this session.

The question, "What's on your mind?" is also a great way to begin. Other options include, "What would you like to focus on today?" Or, "What do you need most from our coaching session today?" The point is to convey that you're there to help with whatever Debbie would like to discuss.

By asking her to take the lead in setting the agenda, you're demonstrating your commitment to attending to her concerns. You're asking Debbie to take responsibility for the outcome of the meeting. And, of course, the two of you are clarifying the purpose of the coaching session, which may vary greatly from one session to the next, and will certainly vary from one employee to another.

For instance, Debbie might tell you, "I need to talk about the year-end project. I can't get the budget figures I need from the accounting department."

When you're coaching Greg, however, he might start by saying: "Things are going pretty well. The only thing that's really weighing on my mind is when exactly the reorganization is going to be announced. The waiting is making me crazy."

And Cheryl might say, "My mother-in-law still hasn't recovered from her stroke. And my teenage niece just moved in with us. So our household's pretty chaotic right now. That's why I've been getting to work a little later than usual."

> **Coaching sessions aren't about advancing your own agenda or ticking off items on your task list.**

Any one of these openings gives you an opportunity to dig deeper, find out more, and offer to help. But for now, this is just agenda-setting time. So regardless of what an employee says, write it down, then ask, "What else should we be sure to talk about today?"

Now, do *you* also have an agenda? Sure. You want to help with the employee's agenda, whatever that is. Your only agenda is your employee's success.

But what about the work you need your team to accomplish? What about assigning new work? What about those reports you need your employee to complete by the close of business today?

You'll get your chance. Of course, if a project is due today, you can certainly raise the topic if your employee doesn't. Just be sure to ask about the employee's agenda first, and leave plenty of time for him or her to answer. Try to assign new work in another setting. Coaching sessions aren't about advancing your own agenda or ticking off items on your task list. Coaching sessions ideally are employee-focused and employee-driven.

2. Link back to prior coaching sessions for accountability – "What has happened since our last coaching session?"

Next, you'll check in to see how your employee is coming along with projects discussed and commitments made in the last coaching session. Yes, a coaching session is a conversation and an exchange of ideas. But it's also about taking action and creating mutual accountability. So the plans and projects that you discussed and committed to in the last coaching session will be reviewed and discussed again in today's coaching session.

You can move this part of the coaching session forward by asking questions such as:

"What's the latest on the Fitzpatrick project?"

"How are you doing with your goal to be a better listener?"

"Where are you on your plans to bring Ann up to speed on the new CRM software?"

Linking back to prior coaching sessions is an integral component of the accountability coaching model. You're also, by asking open-ended questions such as those above, helping your employee uncover more about what's going on for him or her right now.

Now you could just knock out this part of the coaching session by saying, "Here's how I think you're doing on the Fitzpatrick project, and here's what I think you need to do next." But when you take that tack, you're controlling the discussion. And when you use controlling behavior, your people won't learn anything new, or learn how to hold themselves accountable for results.

3. Explore options and possibilities – "What would you like to do next?"

Step three in the **C.L.E.A.R.** model of accountability coaching is to help your employee explore options that will help him or her progress toward goals and commitments. One of the great benefits of being a coach-manager is the opportunity to help people discover new possibilities for themselves.

In this part of the coaching session, your job is to quiet your mind, ask open-ended questions and listen non-judgmentally to the employee's ideas:

"Erik, it sounds like you've made some good progress on the CRM initiative. What's next?"

Or, "What else could you do to achieve your goal of becoming a better listener?"

As you listen to your employee describe the possibilities, summarize to confirm your understanding. Then, draw out more information on options by asking follow-up questions. For example:

"That's an interesting approach, Erik. What would need to happen if you went in that direction?"

"That's a good possibility… what's another?"

"What else have you tried or thought of already?"

And finally, conclude this part of the coaching session by probing the benefits and consequences of various options:

"Talk a little about your plans for how you'll go about that."

"What are the pros and cons of that approach?"

"How does this option relate to achieving your goal?"

Some people, when you ask them about "what's next," just naturally jump right to the problems that are in the way of their progress.

You might say: "Leanne, you did a good job facilitating the meeting last week and getting everyone's input. What else could you do to improve your project management skills?"

And Leanne may respond: "Well, thanks. I put a lot of work into preparing for the meeting, and I thought it went well, too. But I don't have that kind of time every week."

So part of your job as a coach-manager, in this phase of the coaching session, is to help your employee stay focused on possibilities, rather than limiting options by getting stuck on why something can't be done. Once you've completed that task, you're ready to help them identify what might be in the way.

4. Accelerate progress by removing barriers – "What's in the way?"

Sometimes people can clearly see a goal they want to reach or a challenge they want to take on. Sometimes they have a strong desire to reach it or master it. However, sometimes, something is stopping or blocking their progress.

In this part of the accountability coaching model, you'll use a skill referred to as "coaching through the gap." Goals or challenges have been established and agreed to, yet so far, the person has not arrived there. Therefore, there's a gap between what the person wants and the achievement of the goal. Your job is to help them get from where they are to where they want to be by asking about "what's in the way."

Let's say you're working with Phil, your production manager. The first item on his agenda in today's coaching session was a guilty confession: Even though he was planning to create a large public job board to monitor the flow of work through your plant, he has not yet accomplished this task. Here's where you might go from there:

1) *Clarify the task*: How will this move you closer to other goals you've set? Who will find it useful? What will it accomplish?

2) ***Clarify the resources***: What other similar projects have you managed? What materials might you need? Whose support do you need?

3) ***Clarify the timeline***: Realistically, when do you expect this to be completed?

4) ***Clarify the action plan***: What will your next steps be?

5) ***Clarify your role***: How can I best support you?

When it comes to achieving goals, anticipating challenges and obstacles is half the battle. However, notice that you're leaving most of the thinking up to Phil. You're leaving the responsibility in his hands. You're willing to help him think it through. You're willing to help. You're not criticizing or blaming or threatening. You're not even imposing a deadline. You're just asking good questions designed to help him anticipate and remove the barriers, thereby accelerating his forward progress.

5. Recap the session and confirm commitments – "What did we agree to do?"

You might be tempted to end the coaching session after you've discussed the agenda, linked back to prior coaching sessions, explored new options, and accelerated progress by removing the barriers. By listening carefully and offering your own insights, you've helped your employee figure out what to do. But don't stop there! This fifth and last step in the process is critical.

A recap is a summary of what was said, what you both committed to do, and by when. Or perhaps it's easier to remember it this way: play it back and play it forward. The "play it back" part of the recap confirms what happened in the conversation. The "play it forward" part confirms the action plan and where each of you will go from here.

Though it may seem obvious, you'll find, as you begin to use this valuable tool, that what one person says or intends to say is not necessarily what the other person hears. Often, two people in the same room won't hear exactly the same thing. Or you'll find that an important piece of information was left out of the notes you were taking. Or you'll learn that upon reflection, it doesn't sound like such a good idea after all. There is tremendous power in the recap, and I rarely end a conversation regarding any sort of plan without recapping what was said.

Consider what happens without a recap. On Monday, you asked Tom to provide you with a budget for a customer appreciation event by Friday. He says, "Okay." Friday comes and goes. Monday rolls around and when you see Tom, you say, "Tom, I haven't seen the budget come across my desk yet."

> **What one person says or intends to say is not necessarily what the other person hears.**

Tom says, "Budget?"

"Yes," you say. "Remember? We talked about it a week ago. My understanding was that you would get the budget to me by last Friday."

"Oh!" he says. "I thought you meant *this* Friday. Can I have until at least Wednesday?"

"Okay," you say. Come Wednesday, there's still no budget from Tom. You approach him. "How's the budget coming?"

"Oh, right, I finished it, but there was no need to print it out," he says. "It's going to be the same as last year. Except for those few changes we discussed. So I didn't think you'd need to see it."

Is he trying to avoid the assignment, or is he just confused? Either way, you'd have had a greater chance for success if you had recapped the agreement in the first place: "So my understanding is that you'll get me a hard copy of the budget by this Friday, even if it's similar to last year's. Is that correct?"

You've heard people say, "Don't try this at home." Well, in this case, *do* try this at home! Your spouse or partner calls you at work, asks you to pick up the dry cleaning, pick up the two older kids, and pick up some Chinese food on the way home from work.

Great opportunity for a recap: "Let's see. That's dry cleaning, Justin and Gavin, and Chinese food. Do you think we should get wonton soup or egg drop soup?" You're much more likely to arrive home with the right clothing, kids and food if you take a moment to confirm what was said. The recap also offers an excellent opportunity to modify the request slightly for further clarification.

In the workplace, I recommend that you discuss recap with your employee up front: "I like to summarize most conversations at the end with a recap, just to make sure we're on the same page, okay?" Otherwise, when you start recapping at the end of a conversation, people might take offense: "What, do you think I'm stupid? Of course I heard you." They also might think *you're* a little slow, but don't worry about that. Soon enough, a recap will lead to an important clarification—"Oh no, I didn't mean Terry Geller, I meant Terry Madison!"—that will justify the recap and demonstrate its importance.

I find it useful to ask both "play forward" and "play back" questions when recapping. *What did we agree to? Okay, and therefore, what are we each going to do?*

In the previous chapter, we talked about the "48" as an important part of the structure of regular accountability coaching. Within 48 hours *after* the coaching session, your employee will email you a written summary of the session. However, this verbal recap *during* the session is the first step in clarifying what you discussed, decided and committed to do. The 48 then solidifies those actions and commitments. The recap and the 48 supplement each other, but neither takes the place of the other.

The final element of an accountability coaching session is to schedule the next session. You've probably heard the saying that "little gets done unless you put it in your calendar or your checkbook." If you don't schedule your next meeting before leaving this meeting, you're much more likely to postpone getting together. And, as you know, getting together on a regular basis is essential for making The Accountability System work.

The C.L.E.A.R. Coaching Agenda

In addition to using the C.L.E.A.R. coaching model as a framework to guide the coaching discussion, many of my clients also use the C.L.E.A.R. Coaching Agenda shown on the next page. This form helps to structure and steer the first two steps of the coaching session: (1) clarifying the agenda and (2) linking back to prior coaching sessions. The C.L.E.A.R. Coaching Agenda gives both you and the person you're coaching a fast, easy way to pinpoint items for discussion.

Let's walk through how it works in an actual coaching session.

C.L.E.A.R. COACHING AGENDA   Employee:

Progress Report for Managers

Your performance is based on the performance of your people.

Coaching Check-Ins and Ratings (On a scale of 1 – 10)	For the Coaching Session Dated:						
Your General Status (Coachee):							
Our Relationship (Coach and Coachee):							
Employee 1 Performance/Development							
Employee 2 Performance/Development							
Employee 3 Performance/Development							
Employee 4 Performance/Development							
Employee 5 Performance/Development							
Employee 6 Performance/Development							

Agenda/Level of Consciousness

Clarify the goals for the coaching session ● Link back to prior coaching sessions

(Source Documents: Assessments, Performance Reviews, 360 Feedback, Coaching Sessions, 48/24, etc.)

Coaching Areas of Focus and Ratings (On a scale of 1 – 10)	For the Coaching Session Dated:						
#1:							
#2:							
#3:							
#4:							
#5:							
#6:							
#7:							
#8:							

◆———— **What's the Evidence?** ————◆

You can download a copy of this form at
www.tandem-partners.com

Progress Report for Managers

You'll see that the top half of the form is labeled "Progress Report for Managers." When your employees are supervisors themselves, much of what they bring to a coaching session will be about the people *they* manage. (After all, their performance is based on the performance of their people.)

On the top line, under the heading, "For the Coaching Session Dated:" fill in today's date. You'll be using this same form for a number of coaching sessions, so that you can track progress over time.

Let's assume that in today's session, you're coaching Grady, an employee who supervises three other people. On the left hand side, next to "Employee 1," "Employee 2," and so forth, write in the names of the people Grady supervises: Judy, Lorraine and Peter.

Next, get the ball rolling by asking Grady about his general status. "How are you, Grady? On a scale of one to 10, how are you feeling about yourself and your work?" If things couldn't be better, Grady will give himself a nine or 10. If things could be improved, Grady will give himself a lower number.

Then, ask about the relationship between the two of you: "Grady, how are we doing? How well am I supporting you in working toward your goals? On a scale of one to 10, how would you rate our relationship right now?"

Okay, we're all warmed up. Let's continue proceeding down that left-hand column to check in with Grady on his employees. You'll notice that the assessment boxes for Grady's employees are split in two. The upper half is for current **performance**. The lower half is for longer-term **development**. Give each employee two scores, again, on a scale of one to 10:

"How is Judy doing with her performance? Nine? Terrific. What about her development? Four? Okay, we'll talk about that in a minute.

"How about Lorraine's performance? Eight? Great. She continues to improve, doesn't she? How about Lorraine's development? Peter's performance? Peter's development?"

Completing the agenda should not take a lot of time. It's a conversation-starter and an agenda-setter, not an answer in itself. Don't ponder too long about whether a particular rating is a four or a five. Either number will convey that an area may need attention during the coaching session.

Level of Consciousness

On the bottom half of the form, you'll see a section titled "Level of Consciousness." These are items that your employee is currently working on. They may be performance goals, such as increasing customer retention or improving on-time delivery. They may be current or long-term projects, such as creating next year's budget or developing an employee training program. Or they may be skills your employee wants to develop, such as improving listening skills, or facilitating meetings.

These coaching areas of focus can come from multiple sources: performance reviews, the goal setting process, leadership assessments, other feedback instruments, or from past coaching sessions. You even may transfer an item or two from the employee's 48 form (the "play back" of your last coaching session) or the 24 form (the "play forward" for this session).

Whatever it is that your employee most wants to keep top of mind, whatever he or she most wants to maintain at a "level of consciousness," list those items here. Then, check in to see how he or she is coming along with each of the items. As your employee rates each area, ask for evidence or examples that support the rating:

"Grady, how would you rate your listening skills since we last met? An eight? That's terrific. I see that in our last session you gave yourself a six. What specifically has improved in this area? Can you give me an example of a situation in which your listening was at its best?"

In this way, you're giving Grady an opportunity to think out loud about why he has rated himself an eight. This enhances his learning and maintains a level of consciousness about his coaching areas of focus. While you're discussing each item with Grady, be sure to note anything that requires more in-depth discussion during today's coaching session.

Remember, you'll be using this same form for six or seven coaching sessions (a period of about two-and-a-half months), so that you and your employee can track progress. Over time, you'll be able to compare numbers across the chart. If Grady consistently rates himself an eight in improving listening skills and then suddenly drops to a five, you'll want to discuss what's going on.

And that's the purpose of the C.L.E.A.R. Coaching Agenda: to help you identify areas you can discuss with the person you're coaching. It's a quick way to check in, set the agenda, and ensure continuity and focus from session to session.

In Appendix D you'll find an example of a completed C.L.E.A.R. Coaching Agenda created in actual coach-manager/employee sessions. You also can download a blank form for your own use at www.tandem-partners.com.

CHAPTER FIFTEEN

Upfront Agreements

"Understanding is a two-way street."
– Eleanor Roosevelt (1884-1962), First Lady of
the United States and noted humanitarian

No matter how you mix and match the other tools and techniques you'll read about in this book, you need three things to be successful in implementing The Accountability System:

1) **R**egularly Scheduled Accountability Coaching
2) **U**pfront Agreements
3) **G**oals: Destination Goals and Journey Goals

Note that this acronym spells "RUG." Think of these three things as the foundation; the soft, but supportive and protective bottom layer on which everything else rests. If you care to build on this foundation, by using The Accountability Binder, the 48/24 system, and other techniques described later on, it will enhance your success in implementing The Accountability System. But everything is supported by the RUG.

So let's talk next about the Upfront Agreement, a tool that has generated more buzz than anything else I offer my clients.

The managers and leaders I've worked with use it, refer to it, revise it, and teach their employees how to use it with *their* employees. Some take it home to their spouses and children and use it there, too. Just about everyone I've worked with raves about the Upfront Agreement and how it has changed their work and personal lives. In other words, they love it.

So do I. Why?

Because the Upfront Agreement helps keep relationships on track.

What's the source of many business problems? People relationships. The Upfront Agreement helps you solve some of the biggest management headaches there are, all having to do with people, relationships, communication and accountability.

The Upfront Agreement prevents many of the problems that can occur in the workplace between managers and their employees. It alleviates doubts about who's supposed to do what. It clarifies expectations. It enhances clear communication.

And there's more! The Upfront Agreement is so powerful that it deepens trust, commitment and cooperation, and transforms workplaces into happier, healthier places to be. Really. All of that! I just can't stress how important the Upfront Agreement is in building relationships and entire cultures of accountability.

From a quick internet search, I learned that the term "upfront agreement" has been associated with everything from technology mergers to mortgage banking to natural resources management to the International Tennis Federation. Usually, it refers to a contract that is designed to prevent later disputes.

When used in the context of personnel management, "upfront agreement" usually refers to one-way communication from supervisor to employee. Check out, for example, this "How to Develop Job Descriptions" guideline from the Congressional Management Foundation: "Upfront agreement on what supervisors expect of staff prevents jarring surprises during staff evaluations and provides guidance as to what the priorities of the office are."

True, no doubt. Supervisors *should* let staff members know what's expected. But how about what staff members themselves expect? What about *their* priorities? Many supervisors never ask.

What Is an Upfront Agreement?

Here's my definition of an Upfront Agreement:

- It's a **pact established at the beginning** of a relationship—or at the beginning of a new phase in a relationship;
- It's an **ongoing conversation** about how people choose to work together; and
- It's a **mutual understanding** about responsibilities, expectations and communication.

A pact established at the beginning of a relationship—or at the beginning of a new phase in a relationship. The exact form of the pact—contract, letter, memo, or verbal agreement—will vary depending on the preferences of the two parties. Ideally, some sort of Upfront Agreement will be established in the beginning of a relationship, to set the stage for success. And keep in mind—it's never too late. I've seen many established relationships, including some of my own, improve dramatically, and thus enter a new phase, when an Upfront Agreement is introduced.

*An **ongoing conversation** about how people choose to work together.* Each agreement is unique, so it's not the kind of thing you can cut and paste from a book. (Though we do offer an example in this chapter, and further samples in Appendix E to help you get started.) There has to be a conversation. You and the other person must talk, listen, discuss, and agree.

Note the word *ongoing* as well. Upfront Agreements can change over time. They're guideposts along the route of your relationship. As your course changes, you may find yourself in need of new guideposts. That's a natural, organic part of the process: to add and subtract elements over time. An Upfront Agreement is a living, breathing document, never set in stone.

*A **mutual understanding** about responsibilities, expectations and communication.* If it's not mutual, it's not an agreement. So it's not only about what you as a coach-manager expect of your employee; it's what the two of you expect *of each other*. Many employees are so accustomed to being told what to do that they'll be pleasantly surprised when they realize, that with no ulterior motive, you really want to create a reciprocal agreement about how the two of you will work together going forward.

What's the content of the agreement? You can make agreements about anything that suits the two of you, but the three things that tend to be most important are responsibilities, expectations and communication.

For our purposes, we'll talk mostly about Upfront Agreements as being between coach-managers and employees. Please keep in mind that an Upfront Agreement can be extremely effective and helpful in more personal relationships, as well. They can also be used between members of a work group. An intensive care hospital nursing staff, for instance, might have an Upfront Agreement that clarifies how all the nurses will work together and communicate under stressful conditions.

> When you have clearly defined the expectations of both parties, trust is developed and sustained, conflicts are headed off at the pass, and things just generally go more smoothly.

In my own relationships, both business and personal, conversations often return to the Upfront Agreement. We review: What kind of relationship is this? What did we agree to do for and with each other? When you have clearly defined the expectations of both parties, trust is developed and sustained, conflicts are headed off at the pass, and things just generally go more smoothly.

When Should I Create an Upfront Agreement?

Obviously, the Upfront Agreement should be created... up front! As a practical matter, you're not going to sit down with every new acquaintance and propose, "Let's create an Upfront Agreement!" But as you begin to implement The Accountability System at work, this is one of the first things you should do with each member of your team.

Ideally, the creation of an Upfront Agreement should happen in your first accountability coaching session, so that you set the stage for how you will work together from here on out. Whether you're new on the job or have worked together for years, the Upfront Agreement will establish the new "norms" for how you'll work together.

What's Included in an Upfront Agreement?

What kinds of things should be included? We'll answer that over the next several pages. But first, take a moment to think about this for yourself. Visualize your relationship with your own supervisor and, then again, with some of your employees. Ask yourself:

- What are some of the things you'd like to discuss about how you could best work together?
- How would you like to communicate with each other?
- What sorts of things would you prefer to discuss in person versus via email or on the phone?
- How would you like that person to help you reach your goals, and how do you think you could be helpful in return?
- What else would you like to understand and clarify about your relationship from the very beginning?

The most effective Upfront Agreements I've seen include most or all of these elements:

1. Intentions in our relationship
2. Responsibilities to each other
3. Expectations of each other
4. Communication challenges and preferences
5. Permission to say or do certain things
6. Commitments and consequences
7. Where, when and how often to meet
8. Confidentiality
9. Making requests; taking notes; summarizing meetings
10. Agreement about using tools like the 48/24

**In Appendix F, you'll find additional detail
related to each of these 10 elements.**

MAKING REQUESTS

One item you may choose to discuss and include in your Upfront Agreement is "Making Requests." As a coach-manager, there will be times when you need to challenge your employee's thinking or convey something important or sensitive. In keeping with the principle of "Ask, don't Tell," I teach my clients how to make requests during a coaching session.

Coach-Manager: "So what I'm hearing is that your discussion with the head engineer didn't go as well as you'd like, even though you covered everything we discussed in our last coaching session. Is that correct?"

Employee: Yes, that's mostly correct. I mean, I can't say we covered *every* point that you and I discussed last time....

Coach-Manager: What do you think might have been missing from the discussion?

Employee: Well, for one thing, we didn't cover the order entry process like I wanted to.

Coach-Manager: Can you say more about that?

Employee: To be honest, I'm not really all that clear on our order entry process, so I felt uncomfortable bringing it up.

Coach-Manager: I'd like to make a request. Before our next coaching session, please go back and review your notes and come prepared to discuss any points that need clarification. That way, you'll be in a better position to discuss it with the head engineer. Would you be willing to do that?

Employee: Yes, I can do that.

As you can see, a request is just a request; it's not an order, dictate or command. You can do it, not do it, or you can discuss it. There are no request police: it's simply what it says—a request.

Your discussion as a result of a request might lead to proposed alternatives, compromises, or other solutions, including better ideas than you were able to think of on your own.

None of these things are possible in response to a demand.

And making requests is reciprocal—just like the Upfront Agreement. A request may come from either the coach-manager or the employee. Making requests gives you and your employee freedom of choice. It fosters ownership of the action to be taken. It also, not inconsequentially, eliminates the risk of controlling behavior on the part of the manager.

You also may feel it's important to address socializing in the Upfront Agreement. Ask your employee, "Allyson, do you like to chat for a while when we first get together, or do you prefer to get right down to work?"

"I like to check in a bit first," Allyson might say. Or maybe she'll tease you: "We'd better chat a bit first so I can tell if you're in a bad mood."

Another person might say, "Let's get right down to work."

If the socializing gets out of hand, you can revise the Upfront Agreement and decide, together, to set a limit on chatting. "You know we share a passion for music, and I could talk about it all day. But how about we set a limit on it, so that after the first 10 minutes we get down to work, okay?" That way, you're involving the other person in the decision-making and respecting their preferences, without allowing them to sabotage the business purpose of the coaching session.

What Will My Upfront Agreement Look Like?

This depends on your personal style and preference, and that of the person you're coaching. However, the vast majority of people I've worked with say that a written Upfront Agreement is better than one that hasn't been committed to writing.

Your Upfront Agreement can take any form you find useful: handwritten, typed, bullet points, sentences, whatever. It doesn't have to be formal, unless that's your preference.

When you create the written document, each of you may wish to sign and date it, investing each of you in the commitment.

Remember, too, that the Upfront Agreement is a living document, subject to change and revision between the two parties as their relationship and needs evolve. So put it in writing, but don't set it in stone.

Okay, I Know What Goes into It, but What Will I Get out of It?

I guess it's obvious that I'm a huge fan of the Upfront Agreement. It has made such a difference for so many of my clients. Here's what some of them had to say about how the Upfront Agreement has supported their coaching relationships:

SAMPLE UPFRONT AGREEMENT

Accountability Coaching Upfront Agreement
Between Tamy Thompson and Jenelle Jones
January 26, 2006

1. We will meet every two weeks at a date and time mutually agreed to; we will schedule our next session at the end of each coaching session.

2. Everything said in our coaching sessions will be held in strictest confidence and will not be shared with other parties unless expressly discussed and agreed to.

3. We will allow each other to discuss any issue, whether business or personal, unless a specific request not to is made by the other person. Nothing is automatically "off limits."

4. We agree to keep discussions on track by limiting "storytelling" during our coaching sessions. We give each other permission to point out when the other is going off on a tangent, so that we can regain focus.

5. We have discussed the 48/24 and have agreed to use it as a working tool.

6. We're okay with taking notes, stopping and pausing to write something down, or asking each other to repeat something. We want to be able to play it back whenever necessary to ensure clarity and make sure we're on the same page.

7. We agree to give each other our full attention during coaching sessions (not looking at our watches or the clock and turning off our cell phones).

8. Both of us can mini-recap at any point in the session. The coachee will be responsible for the final written recap of the session (the "48").

9. We agree that it's okay and encouraged to make requests of each other whenever there is an opportunity.

10. It is understood and accepted that we can modify this Upfront Agreement any time we deem it necessary, as long as both of us agree to the changes.

_____   _____
Tamy Thompson, Coach   Jenelle Jones, Coachee

For additional samples and suggested content for your Upfront Agreement, see Appendices E and F.

"The Upfront Agreement sets the table for open communication. It eliminates the 'excuse' of not being able to talk to your manager about what's really going on. You can get to the root of the issue or challenge more quickly."

"The Upfront Agreement is a MUTUAL process that sets the ground rules for all dealings in a relationship between two people. It's invaluable because it provides insight on how the other party likes to be dealt with ... helps both parties stay away from 'triggers' that could be detrimental to the relationship ... identifies potential problem areas in the relationship before they arise ... helps tear down the traditional 'boss' role ... and can validate people's needs."

"The Upfront Agreement helped create a bond between me and my new employee that would have taken much longer to establish without it."

"The light went on when I began discussing it with one of my key people and we put in writing what our expectations were and how we would handle difficult situations. The act of writing the Agreement together created significant progress in understanding each other. It's also a reference point for our agreement on quality standards and how I am to communicate with her when I feel we haven't met our standards."

"The Upfront Agreement is critical because it provides clarity to the relationship by identifying mutual expectations. It sets the table for honest and direct communication. This fosters development of a trusting relationship between the parties, which enhances the coach's ability to get to those 'breakthrough' moments with the coachee. That's my story and I'm sticking to it!"

How Should I Introduce the Upfront Agreement?

If you've never done this before, approaching your employee about an Upfront Agreement may feel awkward.

Imagine yourself talking to your employee, and see if you can visualize yourself saying something along these lines:

"Dawn, as you know, we're implementing The Accountability System in our company, which includes getting together for regular accountability coaching sessions. In our first coaching session, I'd like to ask you to participate in the process of creating an Upfront Agreement with me. Okay?"

If Dawn responds with, "No, I don't think that's necessary," you'll need to back up and explain more before moving forward.

For example, you may say: "An Upfront Agreement clarifies how we're going to work together going forward. It's a work in progress, so it can be changed any time, but we need to start somewhere. I'd like us to think about what we expect of each other, what our responsibilities are to each other, and how we prefer to communicate. Dawn, have you ever done this sort of thing with a supervisor before?"

> Do what you can to differentiate between past and present, framing this as an opportunity to create an Upfront Agreement that really works.

Dawn will probably say no. If she says yes, say, "Interesting! Tell me about your experience with that." If it was a negative experience, do what you can to differentiate between past and present, framing this as an opportunity to create an Upfront Agreement that really works.

If Dawn had a positive experience, that's great. Either way, by expressing interest in her experience, you're already beginning to demonstrate the kind of two-way communication you plan to establish.

You also might introduce the topic this way: "I don't have a lot of experience with this myself, so please bear with me as we create this Upfront Agreement together. I really want and need your input, Dawn, so I welcome any of your thoughts that might help us create something that's useful and effective."

You also can add, "Here's where I'm coming from. I'd like to use the ACC Model of Accountability, which means three things:

"1) A is for Approach. I'm committed to making sure that when I'm talking with you, you experience my part of the conversation as an approach, not an attack.

> There's nothing "soft" about achieving better results and doing it with greater satisfaction and less frustration!

"2) C is for Care. I'm committed to caring for and about you as a whole person, as well as an employee. This includes listening to you and responding to your needs and interests and ideas, rather than trying to control you.

"3) C is for Clarify. I'm committed to clarity, rather than confusion. And that's what the Upfront Agreement is really all about—clarifying various aspects of our working relationship up front.

"How does all of that sound to you, Dawn?"

She's likely to be stunned, frankly. Many employees don't normally hear this kind of thing. Others may perceive the Upfront Agreement to be too "touchy-feely." If so, reassure them that the Upfront Agreement is, after all, a business agreement. It's about how you'll work together to reach mutually agreed upon goals. There's nothing "soft" about achieving better results and doing it with greater satisfaction and less frustration!

Regardless of how they answer, you're off and running. You've summarized what the Upfront Agreement is and you've shared some of where you're coming from.

By letting them know what to expect and disclosing some information about yourself, you've put the other person more at ease. You've also demonstrated the "care, don't control" part of the ACC Model by asking for their comments and listening attentively. That, of course, is paramount.

> **Remember, the Upfront Agreement is mutual; it involves give-and-take. If it's not reciprocal, it's not an agreement.**

Don't rush the process! To get off on the right foot, take the time to listen to your employees, and modify your approach based on their responses. And remember, the Upfront Agreement is mutual; it involves give-and-take. If it's not reciprocal, it's not an agreement.

What if My Employees Give Me a Blank Look?

They might. And they might frown suspiciously. Or they might come right out and say they're opposed to it. If they don't know you well, or if this kind of behavior is a radical departure from how you've interacted with them in the past, they might not understand what you're doing, or question your motives.

If so, take a breath and don't take it personally or react defensively. If you sense wariness, you might want to ask them about their impressions and their experience with former supervisors. Explain your motivation. Explain that this is new to you, too.

Then, if they continue to respond to your questions with blank looks, don't let that discourage you. Keep in mind that many employees are not used to being asked for their opinions and input. *Many employees have never really believed that a manager cares about them.* These people almost don't know how to be open, because no one has ever encouraged them to be open before. Or, worse, they may have been punished for honesty in the past. So blank looks and even wariness are natural, and not an indication that you're doing anything wrong.

Most people want to grow. In order to grow, we have to try new things. Some of those things will be outside of our comfort zone. Therefore, naturally, growth involves some discomfort. If your employees express discomfort in the beginning of this process, that's a good sign. It shows that they're openly telling you what's on their minds, which is what you want and need for this process to be successful.

What if My Employee Just Refuses to Create an Upfront Agreement?

If your employee continues to say, "No, I don't want to," or some variation on that theme, take the opportunity to demonstrate your commitment to caring, and *keep listening.*

Ask questions, such as:

"What is it about the Upfront Agreement that's uncomfortable or unacceptable?"

"Tell me more about that."

"I see. What do you think would happen if we did this?"

"What sort of experiences have you had in the past that might be influencing how you're seeing this?"

Some of my clients, when they have experienced resistance from one of the people they're coaching, have tried this: "I understand your concerns about the Upfront Agreement. Why don't we just focus on how you perceive your responsibilities on the job and talk about that?"

You can also, at this point, practice making a request: "How about if we try it and see if it's useful? If it's not, then we'll move on. Would you be willing to give it a try?"

If people are concerned that you're going to be asking them personal questions, or that they'll be forced to talk about their feelings, you can remind them that the Upfront Agreement is a <u>business</u> agreement. It's a pact, an ongoing conversation, and a mutual understanding, all geared toward improving your business productivity and results.

Can I Use Upfront Agreements Elsewhere?

Once you get the hang of creating Upfront Agreements at work, you'll find them naturally spilling over into the rest of your life. You already may have some "upfront agreements" in place. For example, marriage involves an upfront agreement ("to have and to hold, from this day forward, in sickness and in health") as does buying a house, adopting a pet from The Humane Society, borrowing money, writing a will, and many other major events in our lives.

Here's an example. A colleague of mine is taking care of her father, who has Alzheimer's. He's still able to think fairly clearly, but they're both painfully aware that the disease is gradually robbing him of that ability. When I introduced her to the concept of Upfront Agreements as it pertains to her workplace, a light bulb seemed to go off in her head.

"That's what I need with my father!" she said. "We've got a will and a living will, but now is the time when I need to find out other preferences he has. If I'm in the position of making more decisions for him in the future, I can refer back to our Upfront Agreement!"

She tempered her enthusiasm with this caveat: "It's a painful subject, and I don't want to needlessly worry him, so we may do this informally and even indirectly, over time."

I applauded her intent and also cautioned that, in a situation like that, you can't cover everything in an Upfront Agreement. Life throws us too many curveballs. My colleague and her father can't possibly anticipate every decision she may have to make on his behalf. And they probably won't be able to revise the Upfront Agreement, as coach-managers and employees are able to do.

What she and her father can do, however, is clarify his wishes, her intent, their commitment, their expectations, and their relationship, all of which will offer guidelines that will help her make good decisions in the future. Just as important, the guidelines will help her father relax, trusting that his daughter is organized and prepared, and has his best interests at heart.

CHAPTER SIXTEEN

Destination Goals and Journey Goals

"In the absence of clearly defined goals,
we become strangely loyal to performing daily
trivia until ultimately we become enslaved by it."
– Robert Heinlein (1907-1988), American science fiction writer

At every level in an organization, employees must have people to whom they are accountable, and activities for which they are accountable. Those activities are clarified and measured via goals.

In your role as a coach-manager, you must know what your employees' goals are, and must participate in helping them achieve those goals. What, specifically, will the employee achieve this month? What does he or she plan to accomplish by the end of the quarter or the end of the year? What goals will help the employee gain needed job skills or work toward a promotion? Through regularly scheduled coaching sessions, you'll keep those goals in the forefront and will help your employees hold themselves accountable to achieving them.

Most companies establish company goals. Most managers set departmental goals. But many companies, and many managers, are not good at following through on their goals.

What's missing from most goals is accountability: *the ability and willingness to follow through on your own promises and commitments.*

> **What's missing from most goals is accountability:** *the ability and willingness to follow through on your own promises and commitments.*

You've probably heard of "SMART" goals. Many of us have been to seminars in which someone reminds us: "Goals aren't enough. They have to be SMART goals." And we have dutifully written down:

- **S** Specific: Must be clearly defined.
- **M** Measurable: Must be able to document success objectively.
- **A** Action-oriented: Must clarify what specific steps will be taken.
- **R** Realistic: Must have a reasonable likelihood of success.
- **T** Time-sensitive: Must answer the question, "By when?"

I myself am a big believer in SMART goals. The problem is that some of us, after we leave these seminars, return to our offices and proceed to work toward vague, un-SMART goals such as "work harder," or "get more challenging assignments" or "be promoted."

Catchy acronyms aside, we can't achieve our goals unless we clarify them, unless we make them specific and actionable and measurable.

DOING THE RIGHT THING

One of the four practices of accountable leaders is that they "do whatever it takes to achieve results without making excuses." But "whatever it takes" only applies to results or goals that are ethical, moral, and legal. If this is not already your approach to life, it probably won't impact you much to have me talk about it. However, if it is already your approach to life, my reminder might support your endeavors to do the right thing. It's not always easy. In fact, often it's not easy. But if you want to be an accountable leader, it's essential.

One useful way to think about ethics is TWA: Thoughts, Words, and Actions should all be in alignment. If that's impossible (those pesky thoughts *can* be hard to control), at least make sure your words and actions reflect your best and highest self.

Ethics are even more important for leaders, because leaders have more influence, and more power. Yet few people these days really trust CEOs to do the right thing. In a 2005 survey, 95 percent of working people said they believe a CEO's ethical behavior plays a meaningful role in business, but only 28 percent said CEOs have integrity (the "Fast Track Leadership Survey on Business Ethics and Integrity" by IMD, *Fast Company* magazine, and Egon Zehnder International).

"Employees are clearly overwhelmingly concerned with CEO ethics and integrity in business today, which is vital to sustaining order in industry and the world's capital markets," said Professor Sean Meehan, Director of the IMD MBA Program. "This is a universal issue.

We are confronted with it by the MBA participants in all of our programs. Managers have very high expectations of their leadership. Leaders need to know where they stand, how to tune in to the real sentiment of their people."

The survey also found that 79 percent of workers believe CEOs are "ruthless in their pursuit of success."

The top reasons workers reported that they want CEOs to behave ethically:

1) Leaders must lead by example;

2) The CEO represents the brand of the company; and

3) Other company officials will follow the CEO's lead.

The most common mistake people make in the goal setting process is omitting the question, "By when?" This was perhaps the biggest blunder I made early on as a business owner, and I've seen it repeated with many of my clients.

Giving people a timeline is not the same as asking, "By when?" I find it's much more powerful and effective if you raise the issue of time in the form of a question. That way, the person responsible for the activity must take an active role in deciding when it will be completed. It reduces resentment and rebellion and enhances accountability—which, of course, is what this is all about.

The second most common mistake people make related to goals is not following up on the time commitment. Courtney says she'll complete the annual report by January 30th, but what happens if it's not on your desk that day? Are you even looking for it? It's not micromanaging to hold people accountable for the work they promise to do.

Many people struggle so much with goal setting and goal getting. Often, when people discover that they're not on track to achieve a certain goal by a certain time, they give up, as if all is lost. They somehow interpret goals as "all or nothing."

> **Don't let the goal setting *process* become an obstacle that keeps you from achieving the goals themselves.**

Because this whole goal setting process is so challenging, I also recommend that when helping your employees to set goals, try not to get hung up on perfection. What do they want to accomplish? What do you need them to accomplish? By when? Is this goal in alignment with the company's overall objectives and values? Are you sure you're both envisioning the same result?

Okay, then. Write it down. Go for it. Report back.

Don't let the goal setting *process* become an obstacle that keeps you from achieving the goals themselves.

Who Sets the Employee's Goals?

Should the manager or the employee set the employee's goals? If you could answer that question for me, I could probably tell you a lot about your managerial style. I could probably accurately predict how your employees respond to you, and even how accountable they are. I could tell you whether you're part of a "knowing" organization or a "learning" organization.

I don't mean to sound overconfident, and I certainly don't mean to sound critical. It's just that I've observed many managers over the years. In general, those who set goals for their employees belong to organizations where management perceives itself as having the answers, and instructs employees what to do. It's all top-down: "Here's where you have to go, and here's how you need to get there. Don't take any detours."

That's a logical approach, actually—except when you remember that you're dealing with human beings. Humans have a stubborn need to be involved in decision-making, to take ownership of their own work, to feel heard and respected, and to think, learn, and grow.

So the managers in those organizations tend to have more difficulty with ensuring accountability than managers in organizations where employees are coached around setting their own goals.

To some readers, this will sound like a strange notion. Traditionally, goal setting has been the purview of management. "Naturally," it has fallen to them to tell their employees what to do.

I have a different experience, however, and propose an alternative approach. I encourage supervisors to guide employees to set their own goals. These goals should be within the guidelines of their job description, of course. They must be consistent with company policy, mission, and values, of course. But when you coach employees to set their own goals, you've taken a giant step toward holding them accountable to achieve those goals.

This is not to say that managers shouldn't have input. If, for example, you're a manager with a team of four salespeople, and you're accountable for a million dollars' worth of sales this year, you'll need to make certain that your team's sales goals add up to at least a million dollars. After all, you know that as a business leader, your performance is based on the performance of your people. So your team's goals are of utmost importance to you.

But your employees each might choose a different sales target, based on what's feasible for them. If you've hired and trained ambitious people, those four targets might add up to *more* than a million dollars. I guarantee you, if they choose the figure themselves, they'll be more motivated to reach it, and also have more faith that they can, than if they're simply "doing what my boss said I must do."

Destination Goals and Journey Goals

There are two types of goals: destination goals and journey goals. Some people differentiate between performance goals and developmental goals, or job performance and career development goals. Those terms point to similar concepts, but my clients find the destination/journey description to be the most meaningful and memorable.

A destination goal is an intended end point. Where do you want to go?

A journey goal is what you must do in order to reach the destination goal. What will help you get there?

For instance, what are the destination goals of a linebacker in football? Making a certain number of tackles, stopping the rush, making interceptions, preventing yardage. All of those goals are quantifiable, and can be easily measured. They all contribute to the team's larger destination goal: winning a game or a championship. For the linebacker, they're destinations in themselves.

Journey goals, in contrast, are not really ends in themselves, but rather, a means to an end. What must the linebacker do to achieve the destination goals? Gain strength and agility, for a start. Learn the plays. Develop endurance, balance, and speed.

Do you see how the linebacker simply cannot succeed by focusing on the destination goal alone? Yet that's what many managers do: focus only on the end game. They forget that their employees need to get smarter, by studying the playbooks. They need to develop their own strength, agility, and endurance, through challenging assignments and practice.

All of these things take time, and are less measurable, but ultimately improve both morale and performance. Employees become more involved, committed, and fully developed as people and as performers.

> **When companies focus only on the end goal, and overlook employee development, they almost encourage stagnation.**

Not only that, but those managers who invest in employee development make a greater contribution to their companies. They're expanding the company's core competencies by helping to create a more capable and mature workforce.

When managers focus only on the end goal, they almost encourage stagnation. If employees are not encouraged to strengthen, stretch, and learn new things, how can they develop? How can your company grow and keep up with the times? If you don't focus on journey goals, at best, you'll only be as good this year as you were last year.

What are some examples of professional **destination** goals?

- Expanding sales into a new territory.
- Increasing annual revenues by 12 percent.
- Recruiting and hiring eight new staff members.
- Cutting expenses by 15 percent this year.
- Winning a coveted award.
- Bringing in 95 percent of all jobs on time and under budget.

And what might some professional **journey** goals be?

- Improving active listening skills.
- Facilitating large group meetings.
- Giving compelling presentations.
- Expanding one's business network.
- Finding and developing talented people.
- Learning advanced techniques for conflict management.

Some of these might be called soft skills. Sometimes that's said in a derogatory way. Yet these are essential steps on the journey toward reaching one's destination goals. Though they're not as readily quantifiable as destination goals, each one can be broken down into small, achievable steps. You might read a book or attend a seminar on the subject. You might practice and get feedback. When you simply identify a journey goal—"I want to become a better active listener"— you've already taken one step toward success, because your awareness will help you focus on achieving it.

The wonderful thing about journey goals is that they're not just useful for reaching a particular destination. They're useful throughout your entire journey in life. Sure, they'll help you get where you're going. But they'll also help you get to places you may never have dreamed of going.

The Sistine Chapel Surprise

Here's a story about destination goals and journey goals in Michelangelo's life. His extraordinary experience might give you new insight into your own potential, and your own path.

From Michelangelo's perspective, the destination goal was magnificent marble sculptures. By the time he was 25, in 1500, he already had completed two of the most admired sculptures in the world today—the *David* and the *Pieta*—and had established himself as a preeminent sculptor. By the time he died at age 88, he had produced at least 300 marble sculptures (some unfinished). Marble sculptures were his focus and his passion, his life's work.

His journey goals were more numerous. Before he could begin sculpting, Michelangelo had to procure commissions, obtain huge marble blocks, arrange to transport the marble from Carrara to Florence, hire helpers for various aspects of this process, and handle numerous crises and distractions along the way. As it turned out, this journey was astoundingly circuitous and difficult. But as often happens with journeys, the challenges along the route forced Michelangelo to acquire other skills—organizer, leader, architect, manager—that would come in handy later.

Michelangelo also took detours, many against his will, which led to other incredible achievements. The painting of the Vatican's Sistine Chapel, for instance, was a five-year annoyance to Michelangelo—a diversion on his path toward sculptural perfection. The chapel's ceiling and its altar fresco, *The Last Judgment*, are "arguably the greatest painting cycle ever undertaken," writes Eric Scigliano in *Michelangelo's Mountain*, but the great sculptor "complained bitterly about having to paint them, insisting that painting 'is not my profession.'"

It was Pope Julius II who ordered Michelangelo to paint the Sistine Chapel. The artist was hard at work on the Pope's extravagant marble tomb when the Pope insisted that he put the project aside to paint the Sistine Chapel. It's hard to say no to a Pope, especially when he's paying your bills.

Michelangelo tried, though. An advocate of his pleaded, "Holy Father, nothing will come of it, because I've had a lot to do with Michelangelo and he's told me again and again he doesn't want anything to do with the chapel, even though you wanted to give him that commission. For such a long time Michelangelo hasn't been interested in anything except the tomb, not painting. I don't think he has the heart for it."

Yet ultimately, Michelangelo did put his heart and soul into the Sistine Chapel ceiling, bringing all of his sculptural skills to the painting project. The Sistine frescoes "mark the fulfillment of Michelangelo's monumental sculptural ambitions, ambitions too vast to be realized in the recalcitrant medium of stone," writes Scigliano. "His ideas for the tomb flooded onto the ceiling."

This apparent detour in Michelangelo's career culminated in one of the world's greatest artistic achievements, and his most popular tourist attraction today. Afterward, he returned in earnest to the tomb project. His quest for perfection had led him to the now-famous marble quarries of Carrara, where the stone was whitest and purest. But on almost every step of that journey, he encountered problems. And each time he confronted these problems, he developed new strengths and skills.

He had labor problems: incompetent assistants; quarrymen who demanded more money; and assorted "cheats," "scoundrels," and "lunatics," as he put it.

Michelangelo had problems with transportation. The blocks of stone excavated from the quarry were enormous, sometimes weighing as much as 15 tons apiece. There were no trucks, of course, and Carrara is not near the river. Oxen, strapped to contraptions made of wood and leather, hauled the gigantic rocks to a long, shallow beach. Then boats had to be lifted onto the shore and dragged, via log rollers, to the rock. Once loaded, the boats had to be dragged back to the Tiber River. Sometimes, all the available boats were too small. One time, several tons of white marble sat on the beach for an entire year, awaiting transport.

He had problems with his supervisors: the Cardinals, Popes, and patrons who paid his bills, but also steered him away from his pet projects. He had problems with weather, plague, mail delivery, and economically dependent family members. His personal limitations got in the way. He was a poor collaborator and delegator; he was mistrusting to the point of paranoia; he suffered from depression and panic attacks.

But the myriad obstacles along his unexpectedly long journey ultimately offered tangible benefits. "The lost years in the quarries did afford Michelangelo a valuable education," writes Scigliano. "For all his weariness and frustration, he emerged from the debacle seasoned and strengthened. He had performed well... managing a large, complex widely dispersed operation. It would serve him well in his crowning architectural effort, when he would design and supervise the construction of the greatest church in Christendom": Saint Peter's Basilica.

Indeed, Michelangelo became an accomplished architect as well as a sculptor, painter, and poet, designing the glorious dome for the enormous Basilica, which holds 60,000 people.

And what ever became of Pope Julius' tomb? Michelangelo worked on it off and on for 40 years. Though its original scope was downsized over time, and though assistants completed the task, the tomb displays a powerful depiction of Moses that ranks among Michelangelo's most impressive achievements.

As you can see from this story, destination goals are dependent upon journey goals. And, our supervisors have a way of leading us in directions we would not necessarily have chosen for ourselves. So does life. But therein lies opportunity. No matter where our journey leads us, we can always take advantage of the opportunities to develop new skills and talents that just might come in handy later.

What are the lessons for you in this story? Only you can say, but please allow me to leave you with these questions:

What's your destination goal at the moment?

What skills do you need to develop in order to achieve that goal?

What journeys do you need to take in order to develop those skills?

What are you learning, or what could you learn, as a result of the detours you've had to take in the past, or are now taking?

And finally, is there something beautiful that you've created, or could create, as a result of an unexpected path you've taken along your journey? What's *your* Sistine Chapel?

CHAPTER SEVENTEEN

Listen to This!

*"It is the province of knowledge to speak
and it is the privilege of wisdom to listen."*
– **Oliver Wendell Holmes, Sr. (1809-1894)**
American poet and physician

Now you know the principles of The Accountability System, the basic elements of regularly scheduled coaching sessions, and have a C.L.E.A.R. model for conducting them. You believe that with practice, you can improve. You believe that the System will help you successfully hold your people accountable for accomplishing the tasks you expect them to.

But since you're dedicated enough to read this book, it's probably safe to assume that just being good isn't good enough for you. You have your own career goals. You know that if you can really get your department to shine, that light will reflect back on you. So *what else* can you do to become a great coach-manager? You can fine-tune your communication skills, the first, and most important of which, is listening.

In many companies, poor communication is the cause of major problems, from production errors to sagging morale.

Often, employees feel misunderstood and mistrustful, despite managers' efforts to communicate and connect.

> So, how do you "connect"? By getting to know your employees and the things that concern them individually. By sharing information that interests them. And, most importantly, by listening.

Why? Employees don't feel listened to or understood. When managers plan to communicate, what they usually have in mind is to talk. They also may distribute handouts, PowerPoint presentations, in-house newsletters, and other forms of "getting out the message." They may hold team meetings—where they do most of the talking.

What all of these strategies have in common is that they're one-way, or mostly one-way. Managers are trying to communicate by disseminating a message, rather than by creating a conversation.

What do employees care about? The same thing that managers care about—themselves. Oh sure, everyone cares to some extent about co-workers, the company, and the company's mission. But mostly we're selfish creatures. When management informs employees of a new initiative, for instance, employees first want to know:

- What's in it for me?
- How will this change affect me?
- What will my future be like?
- Will my workload increase?
- Why didn't they ask me to help or give advice?

So, how do you "connect"? By getting to know your employees and the things that concern them individually. By sharing information that interests them. And, most importantly, by listening.

Think of someone who's a great listener. What makes them a great listener? They don't interrupt. They look at you. They seem focused, nonjudgmental, and willing to help. Can you see how these are also leadership qualities?

In a recent workshop, when I asked a group of managers to list the qualities of a great listener, they were immediately able to call out nearly 50 characteristics!

Doesn't interrupt	Asks if you are finished
Pays attention	Engaging
Doesn't check e-mail	Patient
Asks questions	Allows silence
You trust them	Head nodding
They're confident	Responsiveness
Good eye contact	Sincere
Doesn't appear rushed	Not about themselves
Focused	Asks clarifying questions
Non-judgmental	Approachable
Hangs on every word	Non-presumptuous
Takes it in	Reinforce
Absorbs it	Sensitivity
Makes me feel comfortable	Secure with self
No competition	Accessibility
Here to help	Understanding
Eliminates bias	Shows concern
No assumptions	Non-threatening
Confidentiality	Avoids external circumstances
Present in the moment	Takes notes
Body language	Interacts with you
Ego-less	Encourages you to speak

These qualities are known and highly desirable. Yet how many of us actually practice them?

> **Active listening is what happens when you're really absorbing what someone is saying, and allowing yourself to be naturally curious and helpful in response.**

Perhaps from your own experience, you know how rarely managers actually listen to the people they're supervising. If so, you've probably also noticed how much we all crave this—at work and at home. Do you truly listen to your spouse or children, parents or friends? What happens when you do?

Active listening is engaged, involved, attentive listening. It includes asking good questions, nodding, indicating interest with facial expressions, and listening non-judgmentally. First and foremost, it's a process of discovery: what is the other person trying to communicate?

Active listening is what happens when you're really absorbing what someone is saying, and allowing yourself to be naturally curious and helpful in response—as opposed to hearing them while simultaneously constructing your own response in your head.

Active listening is a profound, powerful tool. It can transform your relationship with your employees, which in turn can transform their commitment to you and the organization. No matter how good a listener you already are, you can improve your skill by studying the art and science of active listening. And, of course, it can also improve your relationship with your supervisor, your colleagues, and your family members. It's the foundation of successful communication.

Because listening is so important, when I teach communication skills, I begin with listening. Sure, speaking skills are important too, but if you don't listen, ultimately, people will stop listening to you. Here are the essentials of becoming an expert active listener.

Focus

To focus is to concentrate your attention in a particular direction. You know that feeling of trying to talk with someone, and realizing they're not really focusing on you? Ever been at a restaurant seated across from someone and notice that they're not really looking at you at all, but scanning the room for someone they know? It doesn't feel great, does it? Yet there are so many other things competing for our attention, it's challenging to fully concentrate on another person.

That's the challenge I set out for you. Shift your attention away from your previous project. Look at your staff members. Focus your attention on them just like a camera lens, zooming in to capture the picture with the greatest degree of detail. Ignore the phones, emails, knocks on the door, hungry rumblings in your stomach, and other distractions. Set aside, too, the doubts, fears, judgments, and other emotional responses you may be having to what's being said. For now, just focus on *them*.

Winkin', Blinkin' and Nod

> If you don't listen, ultimately, people will stop listening to you.

No, I'm not referring to the three little fishermen who sailed off in a wooden shoe… I'm speaking of the non-verbal communication you use to let people know you're listening. It may seem obvious, but smiling, nodding, making eye contact, saying "mm-hmm," and using other non-verbal communication is extremely important to active listening. Short, affirmative statements like, "I hear you," or "I know what you mean" are helpful, too, and let the speaker know that you wish them to continue. The point is to demonstrate, through your body language and short, affirmative comments, that you're listening, you care, and you're fully attending to that person—not nodding off or letting your mind wander.

W.A.I.T.

A few years ago, I admitted to one of my professional colleagues that I needed a little reinforcement myself in becoming a better listener. This colleague shared with me an acronym that she sometimes writes as a reminder to herself in her calendar or on a piece of paper when she's in a meeting:

W. A. I. T.
(Why am I talking?)

Oddly enough, many people, when attempting to listen... talk. We're uncomfortable with silence, we want to be helpful, we have a lot of good ideas ourselves. All of this is legitimate. However, it does not advance the cause: to develop employees to take responsibility for their projects and their decisions. In order to become a great coach-manager, one must first become a good listener. In order to become a good listener, one must first stop talking.

If you know this is a weakness of yours—if you tend to dominate meetings, even when you try to sit back and listen—then keep this acronym close at hand. I like the implied humor of the question; it helps us ask ourselves to "zip it," but in a gentle, nonjudgmental way.

You might investigate within yourself. Why *are* you talking? Habit? Nervousness? Impatience? You might explore where this comes from. Maybe you learned from a talkative parent or supervisor. But it doesn't really matter. Just develop the discipline to be quiet and really listen.

Watch

You're nodding. You're smiling. You're encouraging the other person to continue. Meanwhile, what is the person's body language, tone of voice, and speech pattern saying to you? Watch the nonverbal communication and you'll gain valuable insight into the other person's state of mind and relationship with you.

Is she fidgeting with a paperclip? She may be nervous— in general, or around you, or about this coaching session.

Is he reluctant to look you in the eye? He might be shy, or shy around you, or hesitant to reveal too much of himself.

If someone looks uncomfortable, try to put him or her at ease. Don't assume too much from body language—someone who appears angry might simply have a bad back—but you can get a sense of what's going on, and, if appropriate, you can ask related questions later.

W.A.I.S.T.

Why Am I *Still* Talking? Just a little reality check for you. To develop accountable employees, you're going to have to give them a chance to talk about their problems, their solutions, their ideas, their fears, their failures, and their lives. It won't always be scintillating. It won't always feel terribly productive at that moment. You might be impatient to give answers, give direction, and tell your own stories. Resist these urges. Let go, also, of the temptation to mentally prepare clever remarks or retorts. Just listen.

Recap

This is one of the most important tools in your listening toolkit. As I've mentioned, it's a summary of what you've heard. It should be used at the end of every coaching session, and it can also be useful during the session—as a "mini-re-cap," you might say.

- "I think you just said you're pretty bored around here, and would like more responsibility. Did I get that right?"
- "What I'm hearing is that the steering committee has been difficult to work with. Is that correct?"
- "I think you're telling me this project isn't going to be finished by Friday. Is that the case?"

> When a person hears what they said repeated out loud by another, it often spurs them to expand on their thinking and ideas.

Notice that at the end of a recap, the speaker is always asked to confirm, deny, or modify the statement. Notice also that you're not parroting exactly what was said; you're putting it into your own words, paraphrasing to make sure you understood the overall meaning. The listener benefits by learning that you are willing to put some effort into trying to understand. In this process, not only does communication improve, but the relationship also improves, because the speaker feels cared about.

In addition, when a person hears what they said repeated out loud by another, it often spurs them to expand on their thinking and ideas. Just one more benefit of the recap!

Ask, Don't Tell

When in doubt, don't tell—ask. "What do you think? What's one thing you think we could do now? What obstacles do you anticipate?"

It can seem like a manager's life would be so much simpler if employees responded well to simply doing what they're told. However, that's not how life works. Employees need to be respected, included, and involved. They need to know you care. One good way to convey that caring is through asking, rather than telling.

Good questions lead to such useful conversations and insights that I've devoted the next chapter to them. But don't take this to absurd levels. If a new employee asks where the restroom is, don't answer with, "Where do you think it might be?" Just provide the answer, obviously! But as you improve your listening skills and become proficient at asking good questions, you might be amazed how often your employee comes up with a better answer than you could have—and learns something about problem-solving in the process.

Before we move on to the art of asking great questions, let me do my own mini-recap of this chapter.

Listening is not passive. It's an active way to convey that you care.

And listening itself can be helpful. How many workers really feel listened to by their supervisors? Because listening can improve your relationships, clarify your communication, and empower your employees to solve their own problems, listening is a powerful and effective way to help your employees become accountable for their actions.

It takes practice, but anyone who decides to become a good listener can. Use these powerful guidelines—focus, nod, W.A.I.T., watch, W.A.I.S.T., recap and ask—and I predict you'll notice an immediate improvement in your relationships, at work and at home.

CHAPTER EIGHTEEN

Open Communication Starts with Open-Ended Questions

"The greatest compliment that was ever paid me was when one asked me what I thought, and attended to my answer."
– Henry David Thoreau (1817-1862),
American author and naturalist

Good listeners—and good coach-managers—ask good questions. It takes some practice, because it's the opposite of telling people what to do, which is what many managers think they should do. But asking good questions is one of the keys to ensuring accountability. It puts your employees in the role of authority. It helps them solve problems, make decisions, and take responsibility. It also helps them think, as Socrates discovered and demonstrated long ago.

Here's a story about the power of questions. An anonymous respondent on my Accountability Survey contributed this.

"At one time, I managed a very large paint plant. For every additional gallon of paint we produced,

it fell right to our bottom line—get out more paint, make more money.

A key to financial success was the grinding operation. Therefore, I wanted grinding to be going on virtually 24 hours a day without stop. This required people to really work as a team. Relief operators and raw material folks never let the machine run out, and departments downstream also had to ensure that grinding never came to a stop because of them.

One of those departments downstream was filing. We created a grinding schedule that I made everyone in the entire facility responsible for. I knew if we succeeded with that schedule, all of our other goals would be achieved. Of course, folks in the grinding department understood where they stood relative to the schedule. However, I asked other departments about the schedule as well.

The first day, I randomly picked one operator in filing and asked him how we did the previous day in grinding (which was an unusual question at the time). His name was Barry and he did not know. The next day I went to Barry and asked him the same question. He did not know. However, he did know one thing: I would be back the next day to ask the same stupid question.

The third day, he knew how we did in grinding, and needless to say, word got around the plant. I'm proud to say that grinding output increased 25 percent with no additional capital, and we exceeded our financial goals."

Questions are powerful. They make people think about things they don't usually think about. They almost force brains to wake up out of their daily slumber and consider things anew.

My All-Time Favorite Question

Here's my all-time favorite question, which I've found to be an irresistible opener: *What would you like more of or less of in your work life?*

> **What would you like more of or less of in your work life?**

This is a great question to ask when you're beginning the process of coaching your employees. My clients have tried it and absolutely love it. It's so open-ended that it's bound to elicit some clues as to what motivates, or could motivate, a particular person. I also use this question in the middle of a coaching process, if the person being coached begins to feel listless or is losing focus.

It simply provides a great way to get to know people. Ask your friends, your siblings, or the person next to you on the train. Well, okay, so you probably wouldn't start a conversation on a train that way—but once you're engaged in the process of getting to know someone, this is a great way to dig deeper.

I recommend that you answer this question for yourself, in writing. Later, when working with an employee, ask him or her to answer it in writing, too. Coach them:

"Now's the time to think big, extravagant, wild, and free. This is not a question about what you can afford to do, or what your friends or family think or need or want. It's about you. You can start with the 'more' part of the question, or answer 'more' and 'less' simultaneously, on separate halves of the same sheet of paper.

"What would you like more of? Do three things immediately come to mind? Great. What are they? Make a list. Keep going. Add to the list. Make it six. Make it 10. Don't hold back. Don't censor.

"Now—What do you want less of?

"What is it? Write it down. What feels burdensome or extraneous or limiting? Again, don't censor. Just tell the truth. Even if you can't let go of it; even if you're committed to continuing with it; even if you can't imagine life without it—if you'd prefer to tolerate less of it in your work life, write it down. Then write down some more things you'd like less of. Treat yourself to a few minutes of clarifying your desires in this way."

Now what? These lists are interesting, but what can be done with them? While you wouldn't want to insist, you should encourage your employees to share selected items on their lists with you. They also might want to share the list with a significant other. Either way, it can lead to a thought-provoking conversation, a deepening of your relationship, and a coaching opportunity to help them get more of what they want.

The Three Ws

Let's say you decided to take on the challenge yourself of answering the question: "What would you like more of or less of in your work life?" And let's say that one of the things you want more of is a balance between work and time off. Every year you complain about how you never take a vacation, and you can't seem to get off the treadmill. Now that you've acknowledged that to yourself (and perhaps others), ask yourself the Three Ws:

1) What does it look like?
2) What's in the way?
3) What will it take to get there?

What does it (your goal) look like?

My All-Time Favorite Question gave you a broad outline of the need to take some time for yourself by taking that vacation you've been putting off. Now is the time to add as many details as possible. Where would you go? When? For how long? Who will accompany you, if anyone? What will the weather be like? What will you do? Snorkel? Sail? Read some good books? See the sights? Sleep on the beach? The more you can involve all of your senses, the better. This question is designed to help you envision exactly what you want, which can help motivate you to do what it takes to get it. Again, think big, not small; extravagant, not frugal; wild, not rational; free, not constrained. Can't imagine how the office could do without you for two weeks? *Don't worry about that now.* Just envision your goal, and record those details in writing.

> **What does it look like?**
> **What's in the way?**
> **What will it take?**

What's in the way?

Now's the time to think about what's in your way, whether real or perceived. Is it time, money or commitments? Too many projects on deadline? Need another thousand dollars? Write it down. Spouse not willing or able? Write it down. Can't swim? Could be a problem, write it down. Maybe the problem is just inertia, or inexperience planning vacations, or the need to be needed at work. Whatever it is, write down the things that are stopping or blocking you from achieving this goal. Don't let what's in the way, get in your way. Take the first step.

What will it take to get there?

With the first two "Ws," you clearly envisioned the goal, and you delineated the barriers that stand in the way of attaining that goal. The next step is to create a game plan that will help you remove or neutralize those barriers so that you can proceed. The action steps in this game plan might look like this:

Too many projects on deadline? Plan your time off for six months in the future. Prepare your team in advance. Take a few hours' respite here and there as you clear the way for a longer vacation.

Need another thousand bucks? Spend less on restaurants for the next six months and postpone some new living room furniture purchases. Remind yourself that you'll enjoy a special trip more than fancy food and new furniture.

Notice that the action plan involves compromises, but doesn't necessarily mean scaling back on the goal itself. Obviously, you might choose to do that—spend your time off at home, or go away but stay at an inexpensive hotel. Initially, see if you can remove the barriers without sacrificing anything from the dream. You might be amazed to see that your goal really is within your reach.

You might also be amazed at how much people get in their own way. Consider the case of Susan, a financial advisor at a large consulting firm. Like a lot of people, she came to me with a specific professional goal in mind. In her case, she wanted to become a senior vice president.

"By when?" I asked.

"By the end of the year," she asserted.

"What's appealing about becoming a senior VP?" I asked.

"More money, more status, more responsibility, more challenge, larger staff, my own office," she rattled off.

So far, so good. Susan was clear about her goal and the benefits of achieving that goal.

But when I asked, "What's in the way?" (the second of the Three Ws) she soon realized that the answer was her personal life. This, too, is often true. My clients and I begin discussing their professional goals, and end up discussing their families or health or other personal considerations.

I often feel the way a physician must feel when a patient "presents" with a certain problem—shortness of breath, for instance—and it turns out that the problem is not caused by allergies, asthma, cold, bronchitis, pneumonia, or anything else that might immediately come to mind. Instead, the problem is caused by smoking. In other words, the patient is the source of the problem. That realization changes the course of treatment. So instead of treating the lungs *per se* (though he or she might do that, too), the doctor treats the smoking problem by referring the patient for smoking-cessation classes.

Similarly, instead of discussing business strategies to help Susan get promoted, we spent most of our time focusing on her personal life. Susan was a single parent with four children. She also had welcomed other children into her home: a niece and nephew whose mother was ill; a church congregation member who needed a temporary place to stay; and a troubled teen whose parents couldn't handle him. Susan had a big heart—and no small amount of stress.

To make matters worse, Susan did laundry for the people living in her home well past the age when they could do it for themselves. She also did all of the shopping and cooking for her growing household. In effect, she had a second job running a bed and breakfast at home.

And she served on several boards of directors.

And she was beginning to date again.

No wonder she had not yet achieved a promotion to senior vice president.

As Susan and I "drilled down" with the help of open-ended questions, we arrived at the core problem: Susan could not say no.

This, too, is typical: many business people have trouble delegating their authority. They have high standards; they expect perfection; and they don't believe others can possibly achieve those high standards. So they do it all themselves.

Susan didn't even delegate to her own assistant. Like many executives, she didn't allow her administrative assistant to handle half the tasks she was capable of doing—a waste of human potential.

So I proceeded to help Susan learn to say no: to doing it all herself; to taking on other people's problems; to agreeing to serve on every board when asked; to doing all the housework herself. We set up timelines for resigning from two boards; we set up work schedules for the kids living at her house; we identified tasks she could reasonably ask her assistant to do.

All of this emerged through questioning. I wouldn't have known how to "fix" any of these problems myself. But you'll be amazed, as I have been, that when you keep asking questions such as, "What's in the way?" and "What next step could you take?" people find their own solutions. They already know the answers, in many cases; they just haven't been listening to their own inner wisdom. The role of the coach-manager, often, is to ask enough questions that people finally begin to listen to themselves.

Oh, and Susan? She made senior vice president within a year. And though she still has a heavy professional and personal schedule to manage, she now has time to take in the view through the windows of her beautiful new office.

Open-Ended Questions

My All-Time Favorite Question and the Three Ws are open-ended questions—meaning, they do not lead to "yes" or "no" answers. Any adult who has tried to start a conversation with a shy or reserved child appreciates the difference between open-ended and closed-ended questions. "Did you enjoy the game?" "Did your team win?" and "Did you score a goal?" can all lead to a simple "yes" or "no," after which, the ball, so to speak, remains in the adult's court, and not much was learned or exchanged.

Some open-ended questions that might lead to better results would be: "What did you enjoy about the game today?" "What skill were you working on the most?" "What would you have done about that angry parent if you were the coach?"

One of the most frequent questions managers ask staff members is, "Do you understand?" This is a closed-ended question. Usually it follows a command: "Increase profits by 10 percent, and decrease spending by 15 percent. Do you understand?"

The problem with "Do you understand?" is not only that it's a closed, yes/no question, but also that it's almost impossible to say no to. It can be embarrassing to admit that we don't know what our boss is talking about, or how to accomplish it. By saying "no," we risk looking stupid or incompetent— which no one wants to do.

What do you think we should do?

Because managers know that "Do you understand?" can sound rather blunt, they try to soften it with, "Does that make sense?" Unfortunately, that's another closed-ended question. Either it makes sense or it doesn't. And who wants to tell the boss that her ideas don't make sense?

If you want to know if you have communicated clearly, try this for a follow-up instead: "That's how I think we should proceed. What do you think?" Or, better yet, before offering your opinion, ask for theirs: "How do you think we should proceed?"

Below are some suggested open-ended questions to guide your staff members toward problem solving, responsibility and a good relationship with you.

What Do You Think We Should Do?

Variations on this phrase include:

"How do you think we should handle this?"

"What next step do you think would be appropriate?"

"What are your thoughts on this?"

"What do you think would work best?"

"Who do you think could be helpful with this?"

The intent is to leave the responsibility for problem solving in the hands of your staff members—and to resist your own urge to solve their problems. Sure, you want to be helpful. But the way to be helpful is by giving them problem-solving skills and practice. They'll feel honored, they'll learn new skills, and they'll come up with good ideas that you couldn't have come up with on your own! So before chiming in with your seemingly obvious solutions to their problems, give them a chance to work it out.

| How can I help? |

Also effective: "What would you do if you were in my shoes?" In this case, you're training them to think like a manager. This staff member might already be a manager, or he or she might be a manager in the future. Even if management is not in the cards, it can be helpful to get another perspective on your next step. They'll feel flattered to be asked, and you're likely to get some good advice.

Remember, you're the coach. Think about a basketball coach. Of the 40 minutes of a collegiate basketball game, how many minutes does the coach play?

Right—none. So you're not actually "playing the game" that's in their job description. You're coaching from the sidelines. That includes giving advice as needed, but mostly you're encouraging them to come up with their own solutions. That's how you develop people, and that's how they grow.

How Can I Help?

The closed-ended version of this would be, "Do you need any help?" or "Can I help you?" Not only do those questions call for a limited yes/no response, but they also force the employee, if he or she needs help, to admit, "Yes, I need help." Many employees just don't want to feel that vulnerable in front of their supervisors. They fear that you'll think, *What's the matter with him? Why can't he do his job? Why is he taking up my time, asking for help?*

Reframing the question as "How can I help?" permits the employee to save face. You're assuming that he needs help. Everyone does. The question is just a matter of how.

One manager I know found herself promoted to a managerial role without much experience and without much training. Lynn had to make up her leadership style as she went along, as so often happens. Fortunately for her staff, Lynn held weekly one-on-one meetings with each staff member. On each meeting agenda, she included this final item: "How can I help?"

Later, when Lynn left the company, her staff held a party for her, and began spontaneously reminiscing about what they had liked about her leadership. "I liked your agendas," one employee commented.

"Yeah, we appreciated that you were organized," said another.

"Shoot, we never even met with our manager individually before you came," said a third.

"It was that final question that I liked the most," said the first.

"Yeah, 'How can I help?'" the whole group chimed in. "We loved that!"

How can I best support you?

It turns out that they had already been remarking about this question among themselves. That simple question— How can I help?—had spoken volumes to them about Lynn's attitude and intent. She really was there to help them do a good job, and by routinely and dependably offering to help, she had conveyed her caring and commitment.

How Can I Best Support You?

This question sounds a lot like "How can I help you?" but has an emotional undertone, if the employee chooses to hear it that way. "How can I help you?" sounds pragmatic, whereas "How can I best support you?" might yield answers along the lines of, "Please be patient," or "I could really use an extra pair of hands," or "Would you mind intervening with the director of that other department? I feel intimidated by him."

Say more about that...

The specific wording of this question is deliberate. The word "best" implies that there are innumerable ways the manager might support this employee in this situation. The question calls on the employee to sort through many options and come up with one way that would be most beneficial. So the question includes an implied statement: *I'm willing to support you in any number of ways.*

A variation on this question is the addition of "right now," as in, "How can I best support you right now?" This wording implies that there will be other opportunities for assistance in the future and other forms of assistance available. While focusing on the present, it does not limit the possibility of other, future assistance.

If the employee does not want to "go there" and acknowledge any emotional needs, that's fine; they can ask for practical support instead, or no support. But keep this question in mind, because it offers a deeper level of assistance, and a deeper level of caring.

Say More About That...

This is not technically a question, but it indicates interest, stimulates thinking, and in effect calls for a response. It's an invitation that's almost impossible to decline, and often leads to a deeper and more meaningful discussion. *Say more about that... Say more about those plans and next steps... Say more about how that might work.*

You've heard of the face that launched a thousand ships? This is a phrase that launches a thousand ideas. Try it with your employees, and try it also with family members, colleagues, and at networking events. *Say more about how you got into that field. Tell me more about what factors went into your decision.* It's not a command, it's a request. When you ask people to tell you more, you invite them to continue talking, thinking and sharing. It leads to better thinking and more understanding.

For example: you meet with an employee one Tuesday, and agree that he will complete the XYZ project by the following Tuesday. But when the next Tuesday rolls around, he admits that he didn't even get started. You might be inclined to say something along these lines: "What the heck do you mean you didn't even get started?!"

Try this instead: "Say more about that." Then pause. Let him explain what got in his way. Listen not for excuses, but for barriers that you might be able to help him remove. At that point, you're not criticizing or blaming. You're helping him identify why things didn't go according to plan, and together, the two of you can work to correct it. Keep in mind that you're trying to create a caring, candid culture. If you ask people to be candid, you can't yell at them for doing so. "Say more" is a caring way to proceed.

Here's an example of how I used "Say more" to defuse a situation in a group. It's the kind of thing that could happen with your staff—if you've got some "wild card" players, as I did in this group coaching session.

I was coaching a restaurant executive. He was in his 30s, had nine direct reports and was responsible for about 80 stores in a $50 million territory. That's a lot of responsibility for anyone, and this young executive felt a lot of pressure about succeeding. We were working well together when he asked me to come talk with his regional managers about accountability. He had started coaching them individually, and thought they were starting to "get it," but wanted reinforcement from me, which was fine.

When I arrived, I shared some of what I know about accountability, involving them throughout the day to get their ideas, feedback, and buy-in. At the end of the day, I went around the room and said, "If you're willing, please share with the group one thing that you will take away from this session today."

When I ask that question in a group situation, I'm careful not to make it mandatory. Some people are shy; some are introverts; some can sit through a session and, afterward, simply not be able to articulate anything they've learned. I don't want to put people on the spot. If they don't care to share anything out loud, I do encourage them to write something down. I explain all this as a way to let you know that I went out of my way to give the group permission to talk openly and honestly, and at the same time not to feel pressured.

We started going around the room. The first woman said that she was excited about using the Upfront Agreement with her own employees. The next person said that he appreciated my open-ended questions, and planned to use those when coaching his people. Then the third person spoke. Angrily and defiantly, he said, "This is a crock of s___!"

There was a stunned silence, interspersed with a few gasps and giggles. The other regional managers knew this guy, but still were surprised he'd be so dismissive and rude to another professional.

He looked at me as if itching for a fight. What would I do now? Would I cut him down? Put him in his place? Publicly chastise him? I could feel everyone holding their breath.

But of course I was there to teach—and model—accountability coaching. So I said, very calmly, "Say more about that."

The contrast between his demeanor and mine was so great that it became comical, and people broke the tension with their laughter. I didn't mean it sarcastically, though; I really meant it. I wasn't intimidated. I wasn't backing down. I was just listening and exploring.

How shall we...?

He didn't respond at first, so I repeated myself. "Seriously, that was an interesting comment, and I'd like to know more about where you're coming from." With this, I was able to convey respect and curiosity, without putting him down at all.

Finally, he started talking. It turns out that he was confused about a few of the concepts. Because of this, he felt defensive. Rather than admit that he didn't understand, he became critical, even hostile. All of this became obvious as he talked about the "crock." As I gradually clarified the parts that had confused him, he became more open, and dropped his critical stance.

I use this example because it shows what can happen when a coach summons his or her own patience and curiosity, and reacts from that position, rather than reacting with anger. You'll see for yourself, if you haven't already, that when you're able to stay present like that, and open, and simply explore what's being said, potentially explosive situations get defused, and the whole conversation turns in a new direction. And it all begins with "Say more about that...."

How Shall We...

With this question, you imply that you're going to help. How shall we find the right vendor for this service? How shall we choose a date for the conference? How shall we handle the problem with your assistant? To empower your employees— and to teach them accountability—you'll probably insist that they do most of the work. After all, you're discussing their jobs, not yours. But by asking, "How shall we..." you let them know you're available for some level of assistance.

Let Me Phrase This a Different Way...

Sometimes even open-ended questions fail to bring about meaningful responses.

You: "So, Fred, what do you think would be a good solution to this quality problem?"

Fred: "I don't know."

In fact, Fred might *not* know. He might feel afraid to put forward ideas that you might deem foolish. He might be in the habit of letting others solve his problems, so he hasn't developed problem-solving skills.

> **Let me phrase this a different way....**

In any case, if you're not getting anywhere, you can try, "Let me phrase this another way..." then proceed to ask the same question differently.

You: "You know there's no right or wrong answer here, Fred, we're just throwing out possibilities. What's one possibility?"

Fred: "Ummmm... I'm not sure."

You: "Well, what's just *one* possibility we could check into before we meet again next Tuesday?"

Fred: "Well, I guess we could take a look at the production reports."

You: "Yeah, that would be a great place to start!"

> **What advice would you give someone else in your position?**

This combination—"Let me phrase this another way" followed by "What's one possibility"—will work well in 90 percent of the situations you'll come across. If you're faced with the other 10 percent, you can use this next, almost foolproof question.

What Advice Would You Give Someone Else in Your Position?

People are notoriously good at rejecting advice, but few of us can resist giving it. When you put your "I don't know" employee in the role of advisor to someone else, you're likely to (finally!) get a response of some sort.

You: "So, Fred, what do you think would be a good solution to this quality problem?"

Fred: "I don't know."

You: "Well, Fred, what if Hasan were in your shoes? What recommendation would you give him?"

Fred: "I guess I would tell him to take a look at the production reports."

See? It works!

Now, just for the sake of argument, what if Fred stays stuck in "I don't know" mode and doesn't budge even when asked to give advice to someone else? Depending on the situation, you might choose to:

1. Offer a suggestion, followed by, "What do you think of that idea?" Remember, this is not a game or a trick. If Fred wants your advice, and you have advice to give, there's no reason not to do so—as long as you also make a sincere effort to teach him to solve his own problems.

2. Or, you can say, "Okay, let's think of this as a homework assignment. Please come up with no fewer than three and no more than five action steps we can take and discuss next Tuesday."

Some people just need time to think. The specific number of requested steps helps them focus their thoughts, and not feel overwhelmed by the task.

In Appendix G, you'll find a more comprehensive list of powerful, open-ended questions, including the ones above. I find it useful to review these from time to time, so that during coaching sessions, some good questions naturally come to mind.

CHAPTER NINETEEN

Why Managers Avoid Coaching

"When you have a great and difficult task,
something perhaps almost impossible, if you
only work a little at a time, every day a little,
suddenly the work will finish itself."
– Baroness Karen von Blixen (1885-1962), Danish author
also known by her pseudonym, Isak Dinesen

Do you find yourself avoiding coaching, or resisting the very idea of it? I've been thinking about some of the objections you might have, some ways you might be thinking to yourself, "This won't work here," or "This won't work for me."

The following are the most common reasons I've been given by managers who are trying to implement accountability coaching:

1. I don't have time to coach my employees.
2. I coach all the time so I don't need to formalize it.
3. I wouldn't be good at coaching.
4. Coaching is too touchy-feely.
5. Sounds like micromanaging to me.
6. Sounds like just another management initiative that won't last.

7. My boss doesn't buy into The Accountability System, so it's not going to fly.
8. I don't know what to coach about.

Can you relate to any of these yourself? If so, that's okay. If not, they might apply to the people to whom you introduce this system, so I recommend that you become familiar with the various ways in which people may express their resistance and discomfort.

First, however, let me note that for the most part, people welcome The Accountability System. They question it, as they should. They're wary of all new initiatives that might fail or be forgotten, naturally. They have doubts about their own abilities, as we all do, and a certain natural human resistance to change.

Nevertheless, overall, The Accountability System makes sense to people, and makes even more sense once they begin to implement it. So if you're planning to implement The Accountability System within your organization, expect some resistance and many questions, but don't expect wholesale rebellion. People want to do a good job, and to get along with their supervisors and their employees. In general, they welcome rational tools that allow them to accomplish their goals. And if you expect a lot of resistance, that expectation will probably become a self-fulfilling prophecy.

In any case, here we go with the top eight reasons managers avoid coaching.

1 – I Don't Have Time to Coach

I've heard this objection on quite a few occasions. Sometimes, while conducting a seminar, I'll watch the audience members nodding in agreement and understanding. I get excited, believing that we're all on the same page. I'm thinking, "Surely, as soon as we're finished, they'll go back to their offices, take The Accountability System, and run with it!" Then a hand goes up:

"How much time do you think most managers spend in coaching?"

Then another hand: "I can see how this would be beneficial, if I had more time."

Then another: "This is probably effective in other companies, but our workload here is just too heavy."

Then I realize: The Accountability System sounds good in theory to these seminar participants—but for *other* people. Why? Because they "don't have time."

Time. That's an interesting concept. Who *does* have enough of it, come to think of it?

Here's what I've noticed: when something is truly important, we find the time do to it, whether it's finding time to exercise, or read a good book or improve our golf game. So "I don't have time" is not a very good reason. What it really means is, "I don't really want to, because I don't see the value and therefore, it hasn't yet become important to me."

> **When something is truly important, we find the time do to it. So "I don't have time" is not a very good reason.**

Here's the beauty of The Accountability System: ultimately it will *save* you time. True, you'll meet with your employees on a regular basis, which may be more often than you're used to. But the time you invest in your people will pay off exponentially. Here's what one client had to say about this:

"The Accountability System opened my eyes to the fact that I'm only as good as the people I've got. Everyone says they want to develop their people, but it always seems to be the last thing they get to. Having a structure, through regularly scheduled coaching sessions, 'forced' me to deal with my employees' challenges and goals. We worked on developmental plans that otherwise would have taken a back seat.

"Because of accountability coaching, I've actually created more time in my work life. I've learned how to use the resources and people I have more effectively than in the past. I've been able to let go, delegate more and be less controlling."

Once you start implementing the System, this will become clear to you, too. Then, as a leader in your organization, you can likewise persuade others to invest their time in this process. Before long, the System will become so important and valuable that time will no longer be an issue.

2 – I Coach All the Time, So I Don't Need to Formalize It

That's great. I'm sure your employees appreciate it. Since you're already partway down this road, I encourage you to take advantage of the benefits that will surely come your way when you approach coaching as a discipline and professional skill. Randomly offering feedback in the hallway, in staff meetings, or during performance evaluations can be valuable. And since you already appreciate the value of coaching, I think you're in a perfect position to embrace The Accountability System, which calls for regular, ongoing coaching sessions.

Those regular, structured coaching sessions signal that something important is happening, in a way that spontaneous coaching never can. When accountability coaching becomes institutionalized, communication improves, relationships improve, and the bottom line improves.

3 – I Wouldn't Be Good at Coaching

Coaching is a skill. As with other skills, you'll improve with practice. Which is not to say that you won't feel hesitant or unsure of yourself at first—you probably will. That's as natural as feeling unsure of yourself before tackling a new home repair project or showing up for a new saxophone lesson. Just don't let that natural fear stop you from trying this, or any other worthwhile endeavor.

Acknowledge to your people that it's new to you, too, and they'll probably cut you some slack. In fact, that upfront acknowledgement of your own uncertainty will help set a tone for a relationship in which your employees, too, will feel comfortable sharing their own fears and doubts with you. So you're not a great coach right away? That's okay. If you do nothing more than show up, care, and be curious, you're in the game. Just commit to the process, give yourself permission to make mistakes, and dive on in.

4 – Coaching Is Too Touchy-Feely

What will your employee want to talk about in a coaching session? And what are *you* supposed to talk about? Isn't all this talking awfully "touchy-feely," when there's real work to be done?

Talking *is* work. It involves planning, strategizing, prioritizing, clarifying and committing.

Coaching sessions are not therapy sessions. And they're not social chitchat. The Accountability System is about developing people and helping people take responsibility. At the core of every conversation is your business objective: to get a job done.

So why do people fear that coaching is too touchy-feely? Because it's new. Because it can make people feel uncomfortable. And because it *can* include personal topics.

For instance, a man I'll call Ken was struggling to keep up at work. He knew it and his manager, Patrick, knew it. Fortunately, since their company had adopted The Accountability System, Patrick and Ken had a process in place to help them discuss and solve the problem.

One day at their regular Thursday afternoon coaching session, Ken said, "I probably ought to tell you something."

"Fine," said Patrick. "Remember our Upfront Agreement? We can tell each other anything. I appreciate your confidence in me."

"I'm getting a divorce," Ken said.

Patrick wasn't shocked. He had been managing people long enough to see employees go through many challenging situations. He had observed Ken engaged in long and heated personal phone calls during work hours. He knew something was up.

At the same time, when Ken made his announcement, Patrick didn't know what he should do or say. "I'm not a therapist" occurred to him, but he realized that wouldn't be particularly helpful.

So he began with, "I'm sorry. I wish I knew what to say."

That simple empathetic statement gave Ken the permission he needed to share some more information. He was already separated from his wife, he explained, and they had agreed to joint custody of their three school-aged children. In addition to the emotional toll the separation had taken,

Ken was struggling with some of the more practical aspects of his new circumstances, including schedules, transportation and after-school care, and how to handle out-of-town business meetings. The kids were stressed. Both parents were stressed. It was just plain hard to focus on his job.

Patrick listened patiently. He had known Ken for three years, and knew that he was committed to the job.

"I appreciate your telling me," he said. "We'll figure out a way to help you get your work done during this stressful time." And together, they did.

Notice that Patrick didn't say, "Oh, then, don't worry about work for a while." As a manager, Patrick still needed Ken to do his job.

Patrick didn't say, "I got divorced, too, and I can tell you, you're in for a real doozy of a ride." That would have been insensitive and inappropriate.

He didn't pry as to who was at fault, or what the financial fallout would be, or if Ken and his wife had considered counseling. He might have been curious about those things, but they were none of his business.

He didn't try to be a therapist, or a best friend.

He simply responded honestly, with care, as a manager should.

Later, he asked questions such as, "What do you most need right now?" and "How can I help?"

Later, Patrick offered a practical question: "What could the older kids do to help out?" He also reminded Ken about the company's employee assistance program and some community resources.

But his initial response was simple. It did not require advanced training. It was not touchy-feely. It involved empathy (putting yourself in another person's shoes) rather than sympathy (feeling sorry for them). It was compassionate, but still performance-oriented. It was just real, and just right.

Your response to a self-revelation might feel less perfect. That's okay. Remember, you don't have to be the best or smoothest communicator. You just have to listen, care, be empathetic, and do your best.

I think it's this fear of failure that makes many people dismiss coaching as "too touchy-feely." Men in particular may not be used to sitting down with each other, one-on-one, and discussing personal experiences. We're comfortable watching football together, or joking around in the lunchroom, but many of us don't have the emotional vocabulary to discuss personal problems in a direct and sincere way. I repeat—that's okay! Remember, you're not a therapist, and you're not a best friend. You don't always have to know the right thing to say, or the right question to ask. You'll learn a lot with practice, but discomfort is a natural part of acquiring any new skill.

Stay with it. Be yourself. You'll get better, and no "touchy-feelings" will be necessary.

5 – Sounds Like Micromanaging to Me

Perhaps as a result of having been micromanaged themselves, some managers have reached these conclusions:

- Employees prefer to be left alone.
- Good managers keep busy doing other things besides checking up on their people all the time.
- If managers ask too many questions, they're interfering.

FROM RESISTANCE TO RESULTS: ONE EXECUTIVE'S EXPERIENCE WITH COACHING

Before I met Alan, I was unfamiliar with and resistant to working with an executive coach. However, another CEO kept telling me what a tremendous help her coach had been to her, so I finally contacted Alan after hearing him speak on accountability.

Even after hiring Alan, I couldn't quite buy into the program. I was willing to support the effort up to a point, but didn't want it to take up too much of my time. Looking back, I think I hoped that Alan would somehow magically turn my employees into an accountable team.

And I'm happy to report that Alan did transform my people into accountable employees. He just didn't do it the way I thought he would, with me on the sidelines. He did it by coaching me to be more accountable to myself. By helping me model accountability, and by learning to hold my people accountable to themselves. He did it by giving me tools we could all use to create the right culture of accountability.

When it became clear that I was going to have to become a "coach-manager," I was anxious. It was new for me. I was afraid I wouldn't do a good job, and that I would look bad in front of my team. I also sensed that my employees might be thinking I was building a file on them, and not in a positive way.

However, Alan encouraged me to let them know that this was all about helping them become better managers. I assured them that what we would talk about during our coaching sessions would be what *they* wanted to talk about. My staff started to come prepared every week with lots to talk about. It began to feel more comfortable for me and the people I was coaching. I began to see how effective accountability coaching really can be.

At that point, things shifted in my mind and I made a commitment to making it work. I began preparing for the one-on-one sessions. I reviewed the previous coaching session notes and looped back on things that they brought up in the past. I was careful to keep the focus on them, so that they would perceive me as being helpful and not judgmental.

To this day, I still have to really work on asking open-ended questions, because my habit is to give the answers. My natural style is to pump people for information to find out what's going on—and of course, these sessions can't be like that. It took me a while, but I finally figured out that part of my style was limiting to people. They might be able to act on my answer, but that won't be as helpful as if they came up with their own answers. In that process, they develop their thinking and skills, and that's what I want.

To my amazement, using open-ended questions helped me see that my people often come up with better answers than I could have thought of on my own. I've worked hard at staying more on the "asking" side of the equation, and seeing the benefits, I've gotten a lot better.

One result of the trust that's developed between me and my team is that my employees are coming to the coaching sessions with more sensitive issues, things they previously would not have discussed with me. Some of my managers have even started admitting when they don't know what to do about a particular situation. We've created an environment that makes that okay.

Something else that surprised me: at the end of some coaching sessions, I hear "thank you." My employees sincerely appreciate my efforts, attention, and guidance. I think they're surprised, too. They didn't expect to enjoy our time together so much. But they do, and I do. It's working, and that's obvious to all of us.

Therefore, many managers deliberately don't "micromanage." When first learning about The Accountability System, people who are wary of micromanaging sometimes ask:

"Shouldn't my employees already *know* what to do?"

"Why do I need to meet with them so often to discuss progress and solutions?"

"Won't my employees resent all this interference?"

"Won't it look like I don't trust them?"

Take a look at this Management Style Continuum below, and consider this question: Where does accountability fall on this continuum, which ranges from absentee management to micromanagement?

Absentee Management　　　　　**Micromanagement**

$$\longleftarrow\hspace{6cm}\longrightarrow$$

On the left side are managers who make only an occasional appearance in the workplace, or otherwise aren't available physically or emotionally to their employees. They rarely hold staff meetings, much less one-on-one meetings. They might make assignments, but they abandon employees to fend for themselves, expecting them to accomplish tasks without providing direction, resources and support. Employees conclude: my manager doesn't care.

On the right side are managers who obsess about details, breathe down employees' necks and restrict freedom of thought and behavior. They claim to know all the right answers, and just generally become nuisances. Employees conclude: my manager doesn't trust me.

So which of these styles is more likely to foster accountability?

The answer is: neither.

Micromanaged employees lack the freedom to solve problems on their own, and the space to be creative. They might be productive, but they won't thrive in that environment, they'll resent being treated like children, and they will fail to produce at full capacity.

Employees with absentee managers will flounder, feeling ignored, unsupported, and unappreciated. Nor is it helpful when managers fluctuate wildly and unpredictably between micromanagement and absentee management, as some do.

> **If you're a manager, you can spend time away from your office, but you can't (or shouldn't) spend time away from your people.**

The Accountability System offers managers a way to pay attention and offer ongoing, consistent guidance. It's not micromanaging because it's done in the context of trust, respect, and empowerment. The employee perceives one-on-one coaching sessions as helpful, not hovering; and supportive, not smothering. Employees conclude: my manager trusts me to devise and implement solutions, and my manager is willing and able to help me with that process.

The Accountability System also offers an antidote to the absentee management style that many employees complain about. If you're a manager, you can spend time away from your office, but you can't (or shouldn't) spend time away from your people. To ensure accountability, you've got to stay involved and connected.

Employees conclude: my manager is committed to my success, and willing and able to help me achieve it.

6 – Sounds Like Just Another Management Initiative That Won't Last

How unfortunate that many employees have become cynical, based on past experiences. Let's see—we've been through Mindful Management, we've been through Lasting Leadership, we've been through Stress Less for Success... what the heck will it be *this* time?

Change is difficult, and arbitrary change is even more difficult. Fortunately, The Accountability System is not another passing fad. If you implement it, The Accountability System will "automatically," in a sense, hold managers and employees accountable. It won't be automatic in the robotic sense, but once the System is in place, people naturally become more accountable. It's the logical and inevitable consequence of implementing the System.

7 – My Boss Doesn't Buy into The Accountability System, So It's Not Going to Fly

In an ideal world, you, your boss, your employees, and everyone else in your company would be reading this book, chapter by chapter. You would then implement The Accountability System at the same time, with support from me personally, or from an executive coach I've trained myself.

As you've probably noticed, this is not an ideal world.

So you're more likely to be reading this book after hearing me present a keynote address or seminar, and you're taking the book back to your office, then trying to implement this System on your own. Fear not! That's entirely possible and practical as well.

I'm not worried about your employees getting on board. They'll have their questions, and some of them may resist initially, but be persuasive and they'll soon appreciate your attention and support.

Your own boss is another story. Does he or she welcome your ideas? Is he or she willing to offer you the kind of coaching that you're offering your team? Will he or she even "get it"?

Not necessarily. Bosses have their own problems and priorities, and you can't necessarily bring them on board.

So—will you fail?

> **Don't let another's lack of support hold you back, or serve as an excuse for inaction.**

No! You don't need full support from the person you report to in order to implement The Accountability System. You don't need him or her to coach you. You don't need him or her to coach you *well*. All of that would be helpful, and in that ideal world we fantasized about, it would be required. But don't let another person's lack of support hold you back, or serve as an excuse for inaction.

8 – I Don't Know What to Coach About

When managers say to me, "I don't know what to coach about," my first question to them is, "Well, what's one thing your employee would like to talk about?"

My second question is, "What's one thing *you'd* like to talk about with your employee?"

Sounds pretty simple, doesn't it?

The truth is, sometimes when people say "I don't know what to coach about," what they really mean is "I don't know how to get started."

If that's the case for you, I encourage you to ask yourself the following questions:

- Have you introduced the concepts of The Accountability System to your employees?
- Have you shared your desire to use the ACC Model of Approach, Care and Clarify in your working relationship with them?
- Have you asked your employees to participate with you in regularly scheduled accountability coaching sessions?
- Have you developed an Upfront Agreement with your employees for how you'll work together going forward?
- Have you and your employees worked together to set destination goals and journey goals?

If so, you're off to a running start! When you begin to meet with your employees on a regularly scheduled basis, you'll create an ongoing agenda of things to coach about, all centered around helping your employee move forward and achieve his or her professional goals.

If you're still not sure what to coach about, or feel unclear about the way forward, turn the page for more information on Getting Started with The Accountability System.

CHAPTER TWENTY

Getting Started

"Take the first step in faith.
You don't have to see the whole staircase,
just take the first step."

– Martin Luther King, Jr. (1929-1968),
American civil rights leader

At this point you probably intend to implement The Accountability System, and to become a coach-manager. You're probably highly motivated to hold your employees accountable. You know it will pay off for them, for you, and for your organization. You've got *The Accountability Factor* for a guide.

Now what? How exactly do you start coaching your employees?

If the prospect of scheduling your first accountability coaching session makes you nervous, that's natural. All of us know how humiliating it can be to fall on our faces. And when we try new things, we risk doing just that. But you're probably reading this book because what you've been doing hasn't been working as well as you'd like. And I'm offering you a system that *does* work. So somehow, between the two of us, we just need to make that leap from "I'm uncomfortable with this and I'm going to avoid it" to "I'm going to get started anyway because I want to succeed."

I'll do my part by making it as easy as I can for you. Here are some simple guidelines to help you get started.

Start with the Upfront Agreement

Remember the "RUG"? The foundation for The Accountability System is laid with regularly scheduled coaching sessions, the Upfront Agreement, and goals. So if you've made a commitment to beginning regular coaching sessions, start them off by creating an Upfront Agreement with your employees. It will help you break the ice, put your relationships on the right track and create an atmosphere of cooperation and goodwill.

Upfront Agreements are part of an *ongoing* conversation; they can change over time. So get started now, knowing that you can always revisit things like responsibilities, expectations and communication as you gain more experience working together in this new coaching relationship.

Identify Goals

Accountability coaching always serves a business purpose. So you need some business to discuss and some goals to work toward in your coaching sessions. If your employee already has some destination goals, why not use your first few coaching sessions to talk about journey goals? That's an important part of being a coach-manager: working toward the long-term development of your people, as well as the business results you'd like to achieve right now.

> If you've made a commitment to beginning regular coaching sessions, start them off by creating an Upfront Agreement with your employees.

Did you also know that people who set effective goals have been shown to suffer less stress and anxiety? And that effective goal setting can result in improved concentration and more self confidence? So what are you waiting for?

If You're Uncomfortable in This New Role, Say So

Everyone knows what it's like to try new things, to be nervous, to be unsure. Acknowledging your own uncertainty can actually put your staff at ease.

> **Did you know that people who set effective goals have been shown to suffer less stress and anxiety?**

It's okay to tell people, "Hey, Scott, I'm using something out of this book. I can get you a copy of it, too. I think you'll find it interesting." Or, "I'm trying this out, Scott and I'm sure it's not going to be perfect. I'm going to make mistakes, and probably you are too, but let's give it a shot, okay?" By acknowledging your own fallibility, you give Scott permission to be fallible, too. You make it safe for him to feel uncomfortable, to question, to be in a learning mode.

But don't overdo the "this is new to me" message, either. You want to project confidence in The Accountability System. Otherwise, your employees will lack confidence in it, and even in you. So admit that it's new, and that you'll each make mistakes. Solicit your employees' support and input. Then, proceed with confidence.

If There's a History of Failed Management Initiatives, Say So

Tell your employees, individually or at a staff meeting, that you're aware of a certain level of cynicism because management has tried to implement other systems that haven't worked out. Let them know that it's natural to be skeptical about change, and that you don't blame them for it.

Then express your enthusiasm for this new Accountability System. Tell them confidently that "it's going to be different this time." Ask for their support. Ask also for their feedback. Admit that though you believe in it, you don't know exactly how it will go, and that you need their ideas as well as their commitment to make it work. Establish that coaching is a two-way relationship—which in itself probably differentiates this from failed management initiatives from the past.

Be Prepared

You've probably heard that life is 80 percent preparation and 20 percent perspiration. The more prepared you are, the less likely you will be to feel nervous, and the more likely it is that things will go well. Review this book before your first coaching session. Prepare your accountability coaching binder with some documents, such as your Upfront Agreement, the employee's goals and job description, already included. Practice your opening remarks, something along the lines of:

"Hi, Donna. Welcome. I'm glad to see you, and eager to share what's called The Accountability System with you. I'm confident that it's going to help both of us stay on track, be productive, and stay in touch with each other. We'll be having these sessions on a regular basis, and I look forward to helping you achieve your goals. I see it as *my* job to help *you* do a good job, and also to feel challenged and satisfied by your work. I think this new System will enable me to do that. How does that sound to you?"

Bring Some Opening Questions to Each Session

Drawing on your knowledge of the C.L.E.A.R. model of coaching, bring some good opening questions to help clarify the goals for the session:

"What's on your mind these days?"

"What would you like to focus on today?"

"What do you need most from our coaching session today?"

"How have things been going in your department?"

There's nothing wrong with writing these questions down, so that you can look at them during the session if need be.

Remember also, that the C.L.E.A.R. Coaching Agenda can be a tremendous help in getting coaching sessions off to a quick start. It's a pretty simple matter to ask the person you're coaching: "How are you doing?" "How are your employees doing?" "How are you coming along with the goals we've been talking about?"

> **You must let your employees learn, and ride—and fall off—on their own.**

Keep this truth in mind: you can't empower people by telling them what to do. Much of coaching involves listening, asking questions, and patiently guiding people toward discovering answers for themselves. You'll probably find yourself wanting to tell people what to do. But remember that if you do, your employees will never develop the skills they need, to do the work you need them to do, which includes thinking for themselves and solving problems on their own.

It's a lot like teaching a child to ride a bike. Your daughter says, "I want to ride a two-wheeler." It's her goal. You're there to help her achieve her goal. So you take the training wheels off. You find a flat, soft surface, such as a lawn. You demonstrate bike riding. You stand next to her, hold the saddle, and point her in the right direction. You run alongside for a while. But she's the one pedaling. Otherwise, she'd never learn to ride.

Likewise, you must let your employees learn, and ride—and fall off—on their own.

One of the mistakes parents (and managers) make is holding on to the saddle too long.

But if you don't make a big deal of mistakes, and don't expect either one of you to be perfect, you can develop employees who eventually ride on their own.

You can even incorporate this commitment into your Upfront Agreement:

I'm not going to make decisions for you. I'm going to coach you to make your own decisions. I'm going to help you achieve your goals, and to do that, I'll be asking you questions and supporting you along the way. I won't ride the bicycle for you. I will run along side of you and help and support and guide you. I expect you to make mistakes. I look forward to discussing those mistakes, and learning from them together.

Has a boss ever said anything like that to you? How refreshing it would be if they did! Remember, *you* can be that sort of boss.

Here's another way to think of it. Imagine helping a child with his math homework. You know how to add and subtract. But is it helpful to the child if you go through each page, saying, "That answer is 11. That answer is 23..." and so on? No, of course not. In order to learn, children have to think, count on their fingers, make mistakes. That's how learning happens.

For students, it requires persistence and a willingness to try. For parents, coaches, and managers, it requires patience, practice, and confidence that the learner is capable of learning. The real learning begins when you let go.

Tandem Partners Leadership Assessment

So you've started coaching your employee Kristina, and you run out of things to talk about. She's up to speed on her work, can't identify any long-term goals, doesn't put much energy into the 48 and 24 reports, and is resistant to your attempts to guide her with the Progress Report for Managers, My All-Time Favorite Question, the Three Ws, or any other ingenious and well-intentioned open-ended questions you may have prepared.

This is a highly unlikely scenario, but just to keep us on our toes, let's assume that you're faced with the above situation. Fine. There are plenty of other coaching tools you can use, including one I'll share with you here: The Tandem Partners Leadership Assessment.

On the next page, you'll see the first section of the Tandem Partners Leadership Assessment©, which is a self-assessment that you, and the person you're coaching, can take to pinpoint areas on which you'd like to focus. The full assessment includes 100 questions in four categories: (1) Executive Leadership; (2) Organizational Leadership; (3) Personal Goals; and (4) Personal Environment. You can download the full Leadership Assessment at www. tandem-partners.com.

Now back to Kristina. First, take the assessment yourself (to experience it first-hand and to set the example), then ask Kristina to take it. In your next coaching session, ask her to identify three items from the Leadership Assessment that she's ready to take action on today.

Notice the phrase I'm recommending. "In which three areas would you like to improve?" is very different than, "What are the three items you're ready to take action on today?"

Tandem Partners Leadership Assessment

What kind of leader are you? This assessment asks you to rate yourself in key leadership areas related to goals, accountability, innovation, planning, communication, customer service, and personal effectiveness, among others.

Part I   Executive Leadership
Part II   Organizational Leadership
Part III Personal Goals
Part IV Personal Environment

This assessment will provide you with a quick "snapshot" of your leadership and personal competencies – areas that need improvement, as well as those you should celebrate!

Part I – Executive Leadership

Please indicate the degree to which you exhibit the following actions and behaviors, using a scale of 1 to 5, with 1 = Strongly Disagree and 5 = Strongly Agree.

		Strongly Disagree			Strongly Agree	
		1	2	3	4	5
1.	I am a positive role model for others.					
2.	I never divulge a confidence.					
3.	I support others when they make mistakes and I help them learn from them.					
4.	I am empathetic and understanding.					
5.	I never flaunt my authority.					
6.	I have a fulfilling life outside of work.					
7.	I create a climate of teamwork and trust.					
8.	I am accessible.					
9.	I give recognition to others for their contributions and efforts.					
10.	I accept responsibility for my own actions and results.					
11.	I demonstrate optimism and positive expectations of others.					
12.	I use my leadership role with firmness or sensitivity, as appropriate.					
13.	I acknowledge and give feedback.					
14.	I help others develop by providing new opportunities for growth and challenge.					
15.	I don't gossip or talk negatively about others.					
16.	I work toward consensus when team decisions are required.					
17.	I don't seek the limelight.					
18.	I let others know where I stand.					
19.	I listen more than I talk in one-on-one discussions.					
20.	I celebrate others' successes.					
21.	I manage my time and priorities to meet deadlines.					
22.	I am always truthful.					
23.	I maintain composure in the midst of crisis.					
24.	I really want to hear other people's ideas and I act on them.					
25.	I always do what I say I will do or commit to do.					

Go to: www.tandem-partners.com
to download the full Leadership Assessment.

Then, in the next coaching session, link back and ask Kristina how she's doing on those three items. Help her craft an action plan (reading, exercises, experiences, coaching) that will help her develop those areas.

"So, Kris, I see you've rated yourself a '2' on 'demonstrating optimism and positive expectations of others,' and you've told me that you're ready to take action on this. How did you do this week? What's one step you can take to improve that rating for next week? What's another step? What else? How can I best support you in improving in that area?"

You can do the same thing, of course, with any items identified during job performance reviews, or from 360 degree feedback, or from other assessments and tools used by your organization. You can do the same with the employee's job description itself. The Tandem Partners Leadership Assessment just gives you another tool to start the coaching conversation, create a level of consciousness around performance and developmental areas, and begin helping your employees reach their full potential.

Implementing The Accountability System Companywide

Unless you own a company, you're working in an environment with a boss and colleagues. At some point you're going to say to yourself, what about everyone else? I sure wish they knew about The Accountability System!

So glad you brought that up!

The Accountability System can be successful when implemented by one middle manager in the midst of a huge company. That manager and his or her employees can grow, develop, become more productive, bond as a team, and thrive—even if no one else in the company has ever heard of accountability.

But it sure makes it easier, and more rewarding, when everyone is on board. So if you share my enthusiasm for this process—or even one-tenth of my enthusiasm—by all means, share this book, and your own success stories, with your boss and colleagues. If your own employees are also managers, please encourage them to do what you're doing: begin holding themselves and their people accountable through regularly scheduled accountability coaching.

Will you succeed at getting others on board? Depending on your role in the organization, and your powers of persuasion, you may or may not be able to convince others to join you. It's certainly worth a try. And if at first they don't seem interested, give it time. Once your team is responding to your efforts, others will start coming to you and asking, "Why is your department functioning so well?" That will be a great opportunity to tell them about The Accountability System.

So what does it look like when The Accountability System is implemented companywide? That depends on the size of your company. I recommend that you begin the program with introductory workshops, followed by more in-depth accountability coaching labs to monitor progress and refine the approach that works best for your organization.

Most important is leadership. The leader sets the tone. Naturally, if the owner or president of the company buys in, then shares his or her passion, that will have a huge effect on success.

If you're the company president, or can enroll the company president in this effort, that person should repeatedly share the message that The Accountability System works. This can be communicated via internal newsletters, companywide presentations, refresher courses, coaching labs, and casual conversations.

One of my clients, the top executive of a sizeable company, gave a speech when a team of his managers attended an Accountability Factor refresher course at their headquarters in 2005. He modeled openness by talking about his own challenges with The Accountability System, and why he was committed to it. Here are some excerpts from those opening remarks.

"You may be wondering—why are we here today? Why do we continue to devote so much time to this accountability initiative? I'd like to share some of my thoughts on that.

"But first let me welcome you, and thank you for the time and effort you've already put into implementing The Accountability System at our company. You're key leaders in this company, and as Alan Dobzinski has taught us, a small change in your behavior can have a big impact on the results you achieve with your team. I want you to know that I appreciate all the changes, large and small, that you've already made—and your time commitment, including your attendance here today. I've become a big proponent of this System, as you know.

"In the past year, we've trained two groups of managers. We have plans to train a third group. So far 56 people have been through the entire process. We've hired a professional coach for our executives. Those executives are coaching their managers. Those managers are coaching their employees. And so on, down the line.

"As some of you know, I've struggled with coaching myself. It's not always easy to be on the receiving

end of it. And when you're used to a different style of management, it's not always easy to step up and become a coach.

"One of the aspects I've struggled with is open-ended questions. I'm not a patient person—perhaps some of you have noticed. So when working with my own direct reports, I'm often impatient to get the job done. I feel like I know how it should be done. So it's hard for me to sit there saying, "Gee, what solutions do you think might work?" I know it's good for their personal and professional development to become better problem-solvers, but it's hard for me. Therefore it's a growth experience for me, too.

"I tell you that, because I know that coaching won't come easily to all of you either. It's new. New things make us uncomfortable. That's natural, and I ask for your patience as we all get used to it.

"Those of you who have been here for a while know that we've tried other things in the past. This is not like those other things. This is not one of the management initiatives that will make us roll our eyes a year from now. I'm committed to integrating this System into the way we do things, and I want you to continue to make that commitment with me.

"I must say I'm aware of the privilege of this System: we're setting it up so that we all get coaches. We all get people we can talk with about our own personal and professional development. I get to talk with Alan honestly about this, and he reacts without judgment. I hope to model that with my own direct reports. I'm

learning from him every day, as I hope you're learning from your coach-managers, too.

"I believe in The Accountability System—not because I want to be buddy-buddy with Alan, or want you to be buddy-buddy with your people. I believe in it because I see it working. I see us not only clarifying our goals, but also reaching them. I see us not only coming up with good ideas, but also implementing them. We're deriving tremendous benefit from this System, and in a way, we've just begun.

"I look forward to hearing from you what's working and not working, and how we can all do better. I like how this is changing our culture, making us more honest, more supportive, and more results-oriented. I look forward to continuing to learn how to be a more effective coach myself—so that I can help all of you do your jobs better, build the bottom line, and build the company."

This executive's comments, and his presence at the meetings, played a key role in integrating The Accountability System into the company's culture. In these opening remarks, he shared his enthusiasm, he humbly admitted his own challenges, and he praised his people for trying something new. This demonstration of commitment helped deepen the commitment of other executives and managers in the company, and I can't think of a better example of leadership.

Feel free to adapt these remarks to your own situation as you introduce The Accountability System to your team, and support them to stay with it over time.

A DOZEN FINAL QUESTIONS FOR READERS

These questions include some review material from the book. You might find them useful for your own purposes, or you might share them with colleagues, then discuss everyone's responses.

1. Accountability is defined as *the ability and willingness to follow through on your own promises and commitments.* On a scale of 1 to 10, how accountable would you say you are, and why?

2. In an ideal world, everyone becomes accountable to himself or herself, and to everyone else. This is not an ideal world. Therefore, someone has to go first. To what degree are you willing to "go first"? If not, what's holding you back? What would be a first step?

3. In order to implement The Accountability System, managers must become coach-managers, guiding the people they supervise to achieve their goals. What, if anything, might get in the way of your becoming a successful coach-manager?

4. As you evaluate the culture of your workplace, would you characterize it as a Have-To Culture or a Want-To Culture?

5. The ACC Model of Accountability includes Approach, Care, and Clarify. Which of these do you do best? Which are the most challenging?

6. If you manage managers, how would you respond to them if they resisted implementing The Accountability System by saying, "I coach all the time"?

7. The three principles of The Accountability System are below. Which of these would be most helpful for you to keep in mind?
    a. As a business leader, your performance is based on the performance of your people.
    b. One small change in your behavior can make a big difference in your team's results.
    c. Performance improves with coaching.

8. The "RUG" is the foundation for accountability coaching. Which of these fundamentals will you find the most challenging? Which will you find the most useful?
    a. Regularly Scheduled Coaching Conversations
    b. Upfront Agreements
    c. Goals: Destination (where you're going) and Journey (how you get there)

9. My All-Time Favorite open-ended question is: *What would you like more of or less of in your work life?* How would you answer that question for yourself?

10. With whom do you already have Upfront Agreements, even informal ones? Who else in your life would benefit from this sort of arrangement with you?

11. Appendix G is full of open-ended questions. Select 10 that you think would be useful to incorporate into your coaching sessions.

12. Another key to accountability success is the recap. (You may have noticed that these dozen final questions are a recap!) Try using the recap at the end of at least two conversations today, then discuss that experience with someone who shares your interest in accountability.

Great Leaders Are Accountable

I hope that at some point in your life, you've been blessed by working for a great leader. The kind of leader who inspired you to see beyond your own limitations, raise your sights higher, and achieve a level of performance you never imagined you could.

Like the very best coaches, great leaders know that their success is based on the performance of their people. They know that without people—without good, respectful relationships with those people—they won't get the results they're looking for.

So they take steps to develop those relationships. They connect with their employees by getting to know them as individuals. They take time to understand the things that concern them personally. They share information with them. Go to bat for them. And, most importantly, they listen to them.

Great leaders discover the best that each person has to offer and then capitalize on their strengths. They help people tap into their own creativity and resourcefulness by providing focus, clarity and awareness of possibilities. They encourage their people to make choices that lead to effective results.

And they hold their people accountable.

Not by using their power or position, but by treating people with respect. By praising them for what they're doing well. By showing them what could be done better. By creating a climate in which people know they can and will make mistakes.

And when their people make mistakes, as they surely will, great leaders notice and correct in a way that's helpful. They openly share the truth about their *own* faults and failings, which sets the stage and makes it safe for others to do the same.

Truly great leaders know their stuff. They take their work seriously—but never themselves. They know the value of discipline. They establish standards, set clear goals, remove obstacles and get out of the way, so that their people can do the excellent job they were hired to do.

Great leaders are great communicators. They listen more than they talk. They meet frequently with their employees. They don't make assumptions about how people are doing. They keep people in the loop by sharing news, plans, ideas, and the big picture.

And they care deeply about commitments. They say what they mean, do what they say and care enough about their own integrity to follow through.

Great leaders are role models for accountability. They know that to hold others accountable, they must hold themselves accountable first. So they take responsibility first, follow through on their promises and commitments first, and accept final, ultimate accountability for results.

If you've never worked for that kind of leader, you might wonder if they really exist. If you're one of the lucky ones who have, you'll never forget the experience.

If you aspire to become that kind of great accountable leader yourself, you can. Just know and practice this truth: The Buck Starts Here—with *you*.

Acknowledgements

Many friends and colleagues made this book possible by generously sharing their insights, expertise and support.

Melissa McDaniel, our Tandem Partner in every sense of the word, provided invaluable organizational and moral support throughout the past year. Her perseverance and good humor was critical to starting (and finishing) this project.

Sharon Kihn, our director of marketing, was a steady presence throughout the writing process, providing equal parts encouragement and critical feedback as the manuscript unfolded.

Terry Weller and our colleagues at McLean, Koehler, Sparks & Hammond supported this venture with patience, consideration, and the space to do our best work. We're proud to be part of the team.

Our Tandem coaches, Sheila Cox, Paula Lowe, Pete Schwartz, Sharon Keys Seal and Anne Teehan, offered encouragement and valuable feedback on selected material, including the C.L.E.A.R. Coaching Model and aspects of The Accountability System.

We deeply appreciate the creative insights and guidance offered by Sam Horn and Mariah Burton Nelson. Thanks also to Marcia Wieder, Doug Stevenson and Sue Bethanis for sharing their adventures in writing and publishing.

Many thanks to our book brainstorming group, Greg Conderacci, Sheila Cox, Patrick Huddie, Sharon Kihn, Milli Pierce, Tim Satterfield, Diane Stahl and Ron Wilson.

Diane Stahl and Sharon Kihn also deserve special thanks for lending us their superb proofreading skills. (Any remaining errors are ours alone.)

We are especially grateful to our clients, who inspired

us to develop a deeper understanding of accountability by asking us the tough questions and having the courage to try something new.

A.M.D. and M.E.W.

To my great friends and hiking buddies, Joel Galvin, Jeff Tuchman, Jeff Schultz and Mark Ford, thank you for your support through this project and through the years.

To my Mastermind Group, Tim Clark, Greg Conderacci, Ellen Fish, Kirk Halpin, John Hennessey, Betty Hines, Todd Levey, Bob Manekin and Mimi Roeder Vaughan, thanks for being such a great sounding board.

To my Mastermind Group for Professional Speakers, Regina Forte, Ben Garber, Nancy Goldstein and Roz Trieber, please know how much I appreciate your ideas and encouragement when this book was just a dream.

And most of all, to my daughter Lauren, who gently prodded me to get this book into print every time we walked into a bookstore: "So, Dad, where's your book?" Lauren, thank you for teaching me the real meaning of accountability with love. I'm proud to show you the result!

A.M.D.

For encouraging my early reading and writing, a special thanks to my parents, Claude and Rose Wiggins.

I'd also like to thank my extended Wilson family in Baltimore and beyond, for many years of love and laughter.

To my smart, funny and talented brothers (not necessarily in that order) Claude, Steve and Andy Wiggins, here's to sibling revelry forever.

And of course, to Ron, Emilie and Trey, I can't thank you enough for your love, support and generous sharing of computer time.

M.E.W.

ABOUT THE AUTHORS

ALAN M. DOBZINSKI, MCC, has more than 25 years of experience as an entrepreneur, executive coach and professional speaker. His mission is to help business leaders achieve their personal best and unleash the full potential of the organizations they lead. Through workshops, writing, keynotes and consulting, Alan Dobzinski is quickly becoming known as *America's Accountability Expert*™.

Alan is a Master Certified Coach, the highest credential awarded by the International Coach Federation, and a designation reserved for acknowledged leaders in the field of executive coaching.

Alan is Director of Executive Coaching Services for Tandem Partners, an organizational consulting firm based in Maryland. Over the years, Alan has worked with hundreds of business owners, executives and managers in numerous industries, including hospitality, health care, publishing, construction, real estate, professional services, technology, manufacturing, distribution, government contracting and non-profit organizations, among many others.

Active in his profession and local community, Alan is a member of the International Coach Federation and the National Speakers' Association and serves on the board of directors of Junior Achievement. A native of Connecticut, Alan makes his home in Baltimore, Maryland.

To find out more about Alan's seminars, keynotes, coaching and consulting, contact Alan directly at 443-589-1153 or via email: AlanD@tandem-partners.com

MARGARET E. WILSON is a founder and principal of Tandem Partners. She has more than 20 years of experience working with business owners and executives on issues related to organizational performance, change management, employee communication and workforce strategy. She specializes in working with family-owned companies and received the Certificate in Family Business Advising from The Family Firm Institute.

Margaret holds a Bachelor's degree in Communication from Towson University and a Master's degree in Applied Behavioral Science from The Johns Hopkins University. She resides in Maryland with her husband and two children.

TANDEM PARTNERS, a division of McLean, Koehler, Sparks & Hammond, is an organizational consulting firm specializing in people strategies that drive business results. Tandem Partners' primary clients are business owners, CEOs and senior executives in companies both large and small. The firm provides coaching, consulting and hands-on support to help clients make sustainable improvements in business performance.

**To learn more about Tandem Partners,
call 443-589-1151 or visit our
website at www.tandem-partners.com**

Appendix A

THE ACCOUNTABILITY SURVEY

While conducting research for this book, I asked a broad cross-section of my clients to take a nine-question Accountability Survey. You might find some of their answers instructive or thought provoking.

1) How do you define accountability?

When people ponder accountability, what comes to mind? My question was open-ended. I grouped the responses by theme.

The Buck Stops Here

That was the phrase used most often. In addition, people who were thinking in terms of ultimate responsibility responded in these terms:

- You're responsible for everything that happens in your little slice of the pie.
- You have responsibility for the outcome and need to meet expectations or be willing to take the consequences.
- Taking responsibility for the ultimate outcome—not just completion of a process.
- Having to answer to someone, even myself, for any project I'm working on.
- Accountability includes a willingness—and more so, a desire—to claim all culpability for those things found unaccomplished—with a commitment to completion.

The Buck Stops There

Interestingly, most people focused on themselves, but some saw the word "accountability" in terms of others:

- For me it means holding others to the same level of expectation.
- Finding out who's to blame, and delivering consequences.

Personal Responsibility

These respondents focused on individual, rather than ultimate, responsibility.

- Taking ownership.
- Owning one's behavior and not being afraid to admit it, to anyone.
- Accepting and following through on agreed actions or responsibilities.
- Taking responsibility for getting your assigned work done.

Courageous Acceptance

The words "guilt" and "blame" came up a lot. Some people also emphasized personal qualities, such as courage, commitment, and congruence.

- You're unable to place blame for poor results on anyone else.
- Courageously accepting personal responsibility for whatever is within your scope of influence even when it is risky, damaging or otherwise a potentially negative outcome.
- Accepting responsibility, admitting guilt if you are guilty.

Universal Responsibility

Some mentioned that accountability extends beyond the workplace.

- Standing behind and representing my truth in every thought, word and action.
- Personally taking responsibility for all actions at all times.
- Successfully embracing assigned roles in life.

Doing Things Well

Some people noted that it's not just about finishing the task.

- Doing things well, on time, and within budget.
- Completing to the best of my ability, and on time, the task at hand, and being committed to that while performing my responsibility.

True to Your Word

These people referred back to the honor of the spoken word.

- Doing what you promise to do.
- Doing what you say you will do, when you say you will do it.
- Doing whatever I say I will and whatever is expected of me in whatever role I am performing, whether it be father, husband, employee, youth group leader, neighbor, etc.

Other Interesting Comments

People must choose accountability:

- In my view, accountability can be proposed and accepted, but not assigned.

For some, accountability is spurred by external responses:

- It's about being able to take credit without guilt.
- It's about completing a task due to expectations of reward or consequence.

For others, it's a deeper commitment to moral behavior:

- Being accountable doesn't always end with things "turning out well." Accountability cannot be "results oriented," or we will become "selectively accountable." The moment that accountability begins to hinge on how we are personally affected... the game is over. Our accountability must not rest on the desire to please ourselves, but on a moral commitment to do what is right.

Accountability leads to achievement, success.

- For me, my tenacity, perseverance and work ethic come from the basic accountability that I feel for my employer but most importantly, my family. Some people do not have this feeling. Those people have no place in my workplace. The positive impact of accountability is that, in most cases, it compels people to overachieve and provide quality results at whatever they do.

- It would sometimes seem easier to escape blame if something goes badly but sometimes being accountable and "facing the music" pays dividends when the project turns around at a later date and comes back on schedule or meets budgets after looking bleak. Upper management sometimes recognizes and rewards these actions.

Ultimately, accountability is good for you.

- Understanding that accountability is something one does for one's own benefit is one of those pesky life lessons that one must learn to become a successful adult.

2) <u>**How accountable are you, on a scale of 1-10, with 10 being the most accountable? Why or why not**</u>?

The average score was 8.5, with a range from 5-10.

Some Proudly Cited Values, Commitment, Standards

- I take full responsibility for my life as it is, for my choices have made it what it is today.
- I usually take responsibility for my actions and the actions of my employees.
- I will step up and take the responsibility for my action or inaction.
- Regardless of demands, I will eventually do what needs to be done.
- For nearly 15 years our business has helped a bunch of businesses, made payroll, and had fun. I also completed over 30 years of marriage to the same wonderful lady. All of that takes being accountable.

Others Cited Reciprocity

- I expect the same for the people I interact with. You can't have one without the other.

...And Various Challenges

- This is an area I have worked on to improve. I am not always consistent in being accountable for decisions that I have made.
- I'm average, unfortunately. I put impossible timelines on my projects, take on too much, and do things too well.
- I sometimes lack focus when presented with multiple tasks.
- I'm a worrier. I take my work seriously, and I get upset if mistakes happen.
- I miss phone call follow-up and mailing dates. I also am too often late to meetings.
- Sometimes I agree to do things that, due to later changes in circumstances, are not achievable. Learning to say "no" earlier to things that are unlikely to actually happen would improve my score.
- Sometimes I am too embarrassed to admit failure.
- I am bothered more than most by my conscience.

3) How did you learn to become accountable?

Most people mentioned their parents. Some thought they were born with the trait; others learned from books or seminars.

Parents

Readers who are parents might take heart in seeing that children really do listen and learn.

- My parents were very demanding about accepting responsibility for our actions. I have always used that training as the basis for my decisions.
- My mother certainly laid on a lot of guilt about not doing what you said you'd do.
- My parents taught me to respect others. If you say you will do something, then you should follow through. They taught me right from wrong.

- I learned from my mom. Whatever she did I tried to do the opposite in hopes of having a better life than she has had.
- From birth, my parents drilled personal accountability into each of the six of us. Our lives consisted of choices we could make and we learned to turn within and trust our inner guidance, as a true guide of what to think, speak, and do.
- My parents set very high standards for their seven children. I grew up eating dinner with my parents and brothers and sisters every night. My father had very definite ideas about behavior and responsibilities and that has carried me through my life. We have instilled the same values in our own children.
- Plain old Midwestern, down-to-earth, do-what-you-say-you-will-do, hard-working parents.
- My father taught me about consequences: there are some things in life you can't control, but control all of the things that you can to avoid unfavorable consequences and undesired outcomes.
- My mother raised me as a Catholic and in an environment that taught responsibility and guilt. My father brought me up through sports and the Boy Scouts, which were also good training grounds. I had a large door-to-door paper route when I was about 10, which was very difficult, and I started working after school and in the summers at age 16 and never stopped. I worked through college, even running multiple retail stores at age 18. I learned early the necessity of, and rewards for, getting things done and it has stuck with me. I have learned that personal sacrifice is part of the game; partially noble, partially selfish, not always as painful as it seems initially, and often rewarded with personal growth and satisfaction as well as the respect of others. The latter leads to success in one's endeavors.
- My parents started very early. I was given stuff to do, then rewards and consequences on the back end (no pun intended).

Personality Trait

- I came from the factory wired this way.

Personal and Professional Education

- An EST-like seminar that I attended in my youth taught me the valuable lesson that we are the true and only masters of our own destiny.
- A combination of education, management discussions, and life experiences teach you that you are ultimately responsible for your own environment and outcomes. Some influential books include *I'm Okay, You're Okay* by Thomas Harris, and *Thoughts on Leadership* by William Hitt.

Professional Mentors

- Our CFO, by being accountable himself, all the time.
- I developed this trait by observing others at work.
- I have had some very good role models in my business life.

Friends

- I have been mentored, taught, and most importantly, held accountable by friends close to me. Through true friendship (the individuals really cared for me and me for them) we have established a level of honesty that at times is hard to take—but has yielded superior relationships and life-long bonds. Accountability is a character trait that has to be honed with much practice.

Combination

- I think it is a combination of my personal characteristics, upbringing, church, and also my first boss out of college. My parents always emphasized the importance of keeping your word and following through on commitments. My first boss was very structured and strict regarding goal setting, planning, tracking, continuous improvement, and lack of tolerance for laziness.
- My parents and professional mentors taught me the importance of accountability mostly through example but also through reminders. I have also done a fair amount of reading on management practices that emphasize the importance of accountability in business and project leadership.

- My parents and my wife. My parents taught me that there are consequences to my actions and to be responsible. My wife reminds me everyday.

4) <u>**How do you hold yourself accountable? In other words, how do you make yourself do what you're supposed to do—even when you'd rather not**</u>?

Public Commitments/What Others Might Think

- There's nothing like the fear of public embarrassment to motivate. So I use public commitment dates (either mine, or someone else's) to drive my scheduling.
- I think of my parents to make myself accountable. I wouldn't want to disappoint them.
- Golden Rule: I ask myself how I would want my staff to handle this situation (if work related) or how I would want my child to behave (if it is a personal situation).
- For those things I don't like doing, I often tell my boss I will do them, which sort of forces me to follow through.
- I answer to my family, my wife, and my daughter and I have high moral integrity.
- Do what I think my boss would do if roles were reversed.

Core Values

- I listen to my conscience.
- Willing to face conflict. Not doing the right thing today usually sets you up for failure in the future.
- My spiritual ideals. A core of good values to do what I commit to doing, even to myself.
- I enjoy being accountable to myself. It is pride that drives me. To meet that standard, I'll do what is necessary to finish a project.
- To hold myself accountable, I remind myself that I believe in moral absolutes, which include truth, honesty, integrity, respect, etc., and that while there are certain things that I am accountable to myself for, my level of accountability primarily affects those around me.

Leadership, Commitment

- I never ask my staff to do anything that I am not willing to do myself. There are always parts of your job that you would rather not do, given a choice, but I'm being paid to do a complete job. I can't expect to hold my staff accountable for their actions if I don't hold myself to an even higher standard.

Rewards/Consequences

- By reminding myself that I'm not going to feel very good if I don't get things done.
- I reward myself tangibly and intangibly for achieving goals.

Practical

- I use a checklist. I review it many times. Especially if it is a project I'd rather not do.
- I am organized, so I set goals, create timelines, and keep track of progress. My goals are usually challenging but realistic so I don't keep failing. Therefore, my track record is good and it encourages me to keep making promises and following through. Practice makes perfect, so to speak.
- I will occasionally seek the encouragement and support of others, usually indirectly.
- That's a big part of it sometimes—doing what you don't feel like doing. Task lists with priorities are good tools. Deadlines are another.
- I identify specific roles in life to which I have either been assigned or have assigned to myself. For example, being a father is a role that was assigned to me. Each year I intentionally ponder each role and analyze how I am doing and what I want to do to improve. I then write that down and review on a monthly basis.

Humor

- I have a self-image that I relish of being a "tough guy"; someone who can get it done and withstand whatever is thrown at me. I talk to myself and tell myself to get going! I get my game face on to avoid hesitation and indecision. Finally, I keep a sense of humor about all of this, including my tough guy self-image. The sense of humor keeps things in perspective so that failures aren't devastating.

5) **In what areas of your life are you NOT accountable? What keeps you from being accountable in those circumstances?**

Not Interested, Not High Personal Priority, Unappealing

- I'm not very accountable when it comes to paying attention to things I'm not interested in doing. I don't send as many "thank you" letters as my mother and wife would like. Mostly, time is the issue, but lack of interest and perceived lack of relevance are close seconds.
- I don't care too much for some tasks and therefore let myself off the hook sometimes.
- Home maintenance—work hours and commute.

Physical/Weight/Health/Finance

- The area I've historically had the most challenge is my weight. I'm accountable for the way my body is, but it seems I often, since parenthood, have put family and work ahead of personal exercise.
- When it comes to personal finance, I have to really force myself to do it regularly. I guess somewhere in my past I was taught that money isn't everything so I don't prioritize that. Not to say that I am not interested in money, but given the choice to do something else, I'll choose the something else and delay the financial planning.
- I sometimes fail in my personal accountability for financial savings and growth for the future. What keeps me from being accountable is a priority shift to short-term pleasures rather than maintaining my long-term vision.

Others' Behavior, Success

- I am not accountable for my grown children's actions or any other person's actions. I raised my children with the same values that I was raised with and I can only hope that I did a good enough job. As for others, such as employees, I can only guide, encourage, and train. If I have done my job, they become accountable for their own actions.

Lack of Consequences

- I am equally unaccountable in work and personal life if I feel I can get away with it.

Work

- I do not always hold myself accountable for decisions I make related to client situations. I have worked very hard to improve in this area and have forced myself to be accountable.

Conflicting Commitments

- Sometimes issues of accountability conflict... a business dinner meeting and your 10th anniversary.

Things I Can't Control

- Weather, economy, how people act around me.
- Some aspects of health. I need to play the hand I am dealt.

Vacation

- I don't really feel the stress of accountability when relaxing with my family, especially when I am on vacation. I tell myself to forget accountability for a few days and just enjoy my family.

6) <u>Are you a parent? If so, how do you teach your children to be accountable? How do you discipline or coach them if they are not being accountable?</u>

Conversation, Repetition, Moral/Religious Teaching

- Constant message that they are responsible for the consequences of their decisions. Allow them to make their own mistakes—but ensure they have to deal with the effects.

- We talked with them constantly as they grew up, building scenarios of things they were likely to confront and ways of dealing with them.
- I am the father of four. My wife and I teach our children accountability by raising them to be adults—not children. In other words, our goal is not to simply coddle them…but to teach and instruct them. Certain standards are set within our household. Things like "do what you say you'll do," "be honest," "be respectful," and "no temper tantrums EVER."
- Yes. Probably not as well as I wish. But, we talk about the importance of others and their needs and the role each of us plays.
- We talk about what God would want us to do in various circumstances. We talk about what happens when they fail to be accountable and when they succeed. We let them fail and learn for themselves. Sometimes we don't say a word but we know they learned. Sometimes we force them to do something they committed to even though they resist. Then we talk about it.

Consequences

- It's great that you used the word discipline in your question. Too often, the word conjures up horrific images when it is used in terms of child rearing. Oddly enough, however, when it is applied to areas like the military or in athletics, people view it as a virtue. Accountability means dealing with consequences. When they're small, it may be a spanking… as they grow older perhaps it's paying for a book that was lent to them that they, in turn, left on the back deck during a rain shower. All of this should yield improvement and gratitude—not frustration—from the child. They are being made better for it.
- With my two-year-old son, I just try to make him understand there are consequences to his actions.
- We have a reward system, with stickers on the calendar or an "X" for bad days. We also use time-outs.

Model Taking Responsibility

- Our focus was always family—we felt that being together as a family was the most important thing. We practiced what we preached. I didn't hesitate to say I was sorry and that we loved them. I do believe in spanking. Punishment was usually some sort of restriction—no TV, no phone, grounded; whatever was most effective for that child. We talked and listened to their opinions. My boys call me daily still, even though they no longer live at home.
- I try to continue to teach my adult child what success looks like. She holds herself accountable. Pretty cool person.

Rewards

- Build a vision... develop a strong developmental process where they can build lots of successes... build loud/ample rewards tied to performance and talk "with" them and not "to" them. Our reward systems beat out any alternate "street" rewards all the time.
- My children are grown and have their own families. When they were little, my wife came up with a rewards program that they both bought into. We really were lucky in the respect that we never had to lean on them for school. They were both responsible students, and had good grades throughout. We kept an eye on who their friends were.

Chores

- We insisted that they work as teenagers and earn their own spending money during high school and college. Also had them set up their own bank accounts early on. Held them accountable for things like being home on time, and paying bills on time.

Financial Management

- We taught one of our children that he had to be accountable for "redeploying" assets when his interests changed. As a teenager, he wanted to quit riding a motorbike and start flying radio-controlled aircraft. We made him sell his motorbike to generate money he needed to acquire his first radio-controlled aircraft. This turned out to be a valuable lifelong lesson. As an adult, he just recently sold a sailboat on eBay in order to make room for new interests in his life.

7) **How do you reward or motivate employees to continue to be accountable in challenging times?**

Varies by Employee and Situation

- Rewards can vary greatly depending on the person and the situation—such as a positive comment, a dinner, a raise, or a promotion. It is important to appropriately challenge the employee and help them to feel successful and part of the team. Financial rewards are more difficult these days but can be helpful if available.

Flexibility

- Increased future flexibility and ability to select the things they are accountable for.

Not Good at This

- One of my weakest areas… I hold a very high standard for myself. I would like to believe that one either holds to a principle or a level of accountability, or they do not. The working world, however, seems to have the perspective that your level of performance and quality is based on your "equity stake." I believe that an employee who performs up to expectations receives a paycheck, gratitude for their contribution, and raises.
- I've made the mistake several times of treating sales reps differently in hopes of gaining desired behavior or results. Now I treat them like adults.

Praise, Private and Public Recognition

- I don't do well at this. They are needy and want recognition. I thank them all the time and send their praises up the food chain to my superiors.... and I let them know I do this. When good news comes from above, I share it with them. They really want that.
- We try to applaud successes in a number of ways, including recognition in meetings and other types of recognition.
- Positive strokes, recognition, and money.
- Praise them. Tell them they have done a good job.
- Public and private recognition when goals are achieved. This includes plaques, awards, bonuses, meals and entertainment, company newsletter recognition. I motivate through contests, leading by example, training and educating.

Financial, Promotions

- The reward systems in my organization are loud, ample, and tied to performance.
- If their being accountable results in more business, or keeping and maintaining current business, they are financially rewarded at an annual review.
- I try to help them by putting them on a career path and giving them positive feedback. I enjoy promoting people and it reflects well on me.

Celebrations and Treats

- We are in the process of setting up an incentive program. As a first step, we have set a standard for monthly collections. I cook or buy lunch for everyone who exceeds the standard. We celebrate every chance we get.
- Buying them lunch, putting a water cooler in, having a bowling party, and taking them out when performance is good.

Written Thank-You Notes

- I send written individualized thank you notes to each of my volunteers twice a year, once randomly and once in November, December or January.

Combination

- Make sure they understand the bottom line impact of what they accomplished: revenue, earnings, customer service, positive impact on others' lives. Celebrate and let them take credit. They need personal pride in what they accomplish. In our organization, getting 30,000 employees paid and caring for 19,000 patients a day is a powerful positive message.
- Employees that have raised the stakes and provided service that you "can't live without" earn "can't-live-without-you" rewards. Days off, vacations, gift certificates to the movies or out to dinner. A more out-of-the-box reward is often a bigger surprise, and if it is customized (such as tickets to see Barry Manilow, if Mandy happens to be their favorite song) it shows the employee that you know them and you want to please them with what's important to them.

Leadership/Vision/Combination

- It's important to create a vision/direction that is larger than the individuals in the organization. People need a reason to get up on a cold, snowy morning and get to work besides a paycheck or generating more profits for the company. It has to have a large self-worth component for each person since WIIFM (What's In It For Me?) is constantly at work.
- We win as a team, and that has both social and financial rewards. In challenging times as well as good times we must keep focused on the greater purpose of the organization. Money is not a motivator; it is a de-motivator if it is deemed by others as unfair.

8) <u>As a leader, what techniques do you use to hold employees accountable for their job responsibilities and standards</u>?

Written Documents

- Techniques include job descriptions, project plans, project reviews and performance reviews using defined roles and responsibilities with occasional reminders.

- We have begun using meeting minutes and other methods to hold people accountable for assignments.
- Upfront Agreements, debriefing, goal reports, and weekly pipeline reviews.
- A daily journal to hand in. Monthly review of activities.
- In my current servant-leader role, I use a variety of tracking techniques to hold people accountable. I encourage people I coach to create clear objectives for themselves and their people—written, agreed to, and signed-off, then regularly tracked and followed up on to assure completion, with recommitment as needed.

Rewards

- A combination of coaching and rewards such as future flexibility.
- Salary increases (for meeting goals); recognition when they "come through" for me.

Punishments

- Disappointment, but not punishment, when they don't come through for me.
- Sticks are only useful as a last resort and are, in my view, a sign of management failure.
- Give them reasons to be accountable, both positive and negative.
- Termination or lack of recognition.

No System/Needs Help

- I really don't have any techniques that I regularly use. This would be a good thing to develop.
- This is an area where our company still suffers. It is now becoming one of our focuses.
- I am constantly looking for new measurement tools.

Lead by Example

- I lead by example. I take responsibility for my errors. I tell them that I expect no less from them.

- I try to inspire them.
- I am honest with my staff. If I can't do anything, I will tell them that; if I made a mistake, I am the first to admit it.

Personal Check-ins and Support; Clear Expectations

- I make sure that I am always available for questions or problems—personal or business related. I review my staff's work on a regular basis and give feedback, positive and negative. I make sure that the staff has all the tools they need to accomplish any task assigned. I believe that you can't share too much information. It makes them realize how important they are to the entire company. And I listen. I may not be able to solve all the issues, but they know that I heard what they said and will do everything in my power to resolve what I can.
- Weekly one-on-one meetings, daily end-of-day review of sales, and periodic sales meetings. Review of commission.
- Mine is a deadline business. Their accountability hinges on meeting deadlines. If they don't, they'd better have a real good reason... and in some cases they do. By and large, they know the responsibility of the job and they are diligent.
- I keep following up with them via e-mail and face-to-face contacts.
- I am a terrible "babysitter." Employees have to either complete a job with timeliness and excellence or come to me—or another company resource—for assistance, guidance, advice, or whatever's required. There are no "points taken off" for seeking help, but it is a huge no-no to fail through autonomy or pride.

Combination

- Don't wait. Tell them face-to-face in a fashion that they can understand, accept and do something about. Emphasize the positives and build on them but be clear about the shortfalls. Allow time for the person to absorb and then listen to them. Develop a plan. Follow up. If they continue to fail, you must either retrain, move to another more suitable role, or outplace in whatever method is best, including asking for resignation, asking them to start looking outside while employed, or termination. Try to be fair.

- I assign roles and expectations from those roles. I then ask lots of questions. "How are we doing on that project?" When do you reckon we will have that? What did Sally have to say about that? What is the future with this account? What's our next step?" If I do not get the answer that indicates the person is accepting responsibility, the next day, I ask the same question. Normally the answer is correct by the third question—and the first or second each time after that. Or in rare occasions, that person might find themselves on another bus.

9) <u>What corrective/constructive action do you take when employees are not being accountable for their quantity or quality of work</u>?

Conversations and Warnings

- The type of action would vary greatly depending on the person and the situation. Actions would vary anywhere from a few motivating comments to dismissal.
- Gently point out how it needs to be changed. As a last resort, do it myself.
- We try to make it clear that we are trying to help train them and change their behaviors in a non-threatening way.
- I first make sure that they have the tools they need to meet the standards that have been set. I always make sure that I can meet the standards myself. I will meet individually with the employee, work with them, and give them every opportunity to succeed.
- If they can't seem to get it, I put someone else in the position to be responsible. The first person might not be a leader, but still a good follower.
- Let them know I am disappointed, and they usually don't want to disappoint me because they respect me as a leader.
- We force the issue until they realize the error of their ways or show us that we're wrong in our assessment. Whenever some-

one is confronted, I need to do a better job of bearing in mind
that I fall on my face *all the time*.

- I ask lots of questions.
- I counsel them and train them.
- Discuss the original commitment and allow them to articulate
the problem and the solution.
- One-on-one meetings; written warnings.

Disciplinary Action

- Disciplinary action and a plan to allow them the opportunity
to get back on track.
- Whippings don't seem to be working anymore, so I now use
techniques like explaining the consequences of what's missing
or wrong; how it will affect the company, the organization,
future assignments, salary, their reputation....

Dismissal/Termination

- Terminate them. However, that's only after several initial
steps to get them on board, plus a "heart to heart." Normally
peer pressure is so enormous that they will leave if they are
not performing. The team reward system is so strong that non-
performers feel worse than awful. That's a good thing.
- Coaching and progressive discipline, up to and including
termination. If written objectives are clear, a person not
achieving them is, in the long term, telling the organization he
or she does not want to continue working there, which makes
the ultimate termination a process of self-selection.

Leadership

- You have to become an enthusiastic, energetic, positive leader.
You need to be realistic but hopeful, and keep your sense of
humor. You need short-term goals that can be attained and
then move onto new ones. Empathy is needed but strength
also. Need to find other "sub-leaders" to help reinforce the
accountability. Reward, in some very personal fashion, your
allies for doing this.

Appendix B

SAMPLE 48 REPORTS

In The Accountability System, "48" refers to the 48 hours immediately following the most recent coaching session. Within 48 hours, your employee will email you a written recap, which will include these items:

1. Play back
   - What was discussed and decided, including goals, plans and priorities.
   - Insights, breakthroughs, solutions uncovered, questions unanswered.
2. Play forward:
   - What the employee will accomplish between now and the next coaching session.
   - Specific action plans: what, how and by when.
3. Additional questions or concerns that have arisen since the coaching session.
4. Parking Lot items to revisit at a later date.

In this Appendix, you'll find examples of actual 48 reports submitted by employees to their coach-managers following a coaching session. (Some details have been changed to protect confidentiality.)

Sample 1– Renée's 48

Recap –

This coaching session focused on my 360 feedback. We chose three items to discuss.

1. We reviewed the positive aspects of item 14 and discussed how to socialize and relax with people and that it doesn't mean I'm not still managing and leading them.

2. We discussed how I sometimes tolerate poor performance and how to begin turning that around by staying on top of it and not letting it get out of hand. I know I need to be more in touch with my employees and what's going on for them.
    *   Action: I committed to scheduling all of my coaching/ check-in sessions with my employees for the next two months.
3. I acknowledged that sometimes I don't do a great job of listening in meetings.
    *   Action: I agreed to be conscious of this over the next two weeks and rate myself privately at the end of each meeting. We will discuss it at our next coaching session.
4. We agreed that we don't need permission to speak more directly to each other and express our opinions.
    *   Action: I will add this to our Upfront Agreement and will send it to you before the next session.

Let me know if I overlooked anything.

Sample 2 – Ben's 48

My notes from our session:

I believe that we finished our first round of analyzing how I manage the budget process. Our future agenda items will move to better management of supplier relationships and other items from my leadership assessment.

Discussion:

1. We discussed the concept of profitability and concluded that we are both on the same page. We both recognize the need to balance and sometimes defer short-term gain for long-term growth of relationships.
2. We put a discussion of cost management in the "parking lot."
3. We had a fairly lengthy conversation about the strength of my relationships with my peers. In ranking from strong and

comfortable to less so, I ordered my relationships as Rick, Paula, Julius, Marie, Matthew and Josh.

4. I committed to seeking out Josh and making an appointment to have lunch. After Josh I will follow with Matthew. Marie is currently on my calendar for July.

5. We discussed my desire to get more people in my group involved in outside organizations and networking. I am becoming active in CDN and have great connections through JPMG. I will get some information on how to become more active with APEX by talking to my neighbor who is a member. We have lost touch with APA, and should get others involved there. APA is a revisit item for our next session.

Sample 3 – Anthony's 48

Notes from today's meeting:

1. Future meeting agendas will include discussion of core competencies; review and discuss leadership assessment; review and update level of consciousness.

2. Client relationships – I will be more aware of responsiveness and appropriate give and take in protection of key accounts. I will organize a system of regular client follow-up. My first action will be to create a spreadsheet that lists the clients I'm responsible for and when I had my last personal visit with them.

3. I will observe myself in setting clear expectations and follow up on same with my employees. I will record examples of these efforts and bring to the next coaching session for discussion with you.

4. I need to better understand if my employees feel they have a clear understanding of my expectations. Do I follow-up well? Am I helpful?

5. I will consider how to set the bar, the target, the goal, without telling.

Thanks for a good meeting. I felt like we got into some worthwhile issues.

Sample 4 – Stefanie's 48

Thanks for what I believe was our best coaching meeting ever. Attached is my updated job description, as well as a final version of our Upfront Agreement.

1. We had a good conversation around the issue of how to receive constructive criticism. You helped me to focus on the outcomes that are possible if I can master this skill.

2. To facilitate this I am committed to taking what I can from comments others make to me, but to not be paralyzed by criticism. I think I understand better now that I have an opportunity to build my credibility in these situations by not overreacting.

3. I will report back to you on my meeting with Don and how I do with focusing on the facts and not allowing myself to get distracted by my own emotions.

4. I also committed to recognizing other situations where I take things too personally, and making notes about those matters and my actions, so that I may understand cause and outcome.

5. We also talked about my management skills, especially getting things done through others. As you know, I am a recovering perfectionist and this is a hard area for me. However, I have made some progress.

   - JP has increased in his production. He finished work on the ABC project last week.

   - CT is doing an exceptional job working through some issues on the XYZ project with very little interference from me.

   - SV has taken on a new role with the company. We've worked together to fine tune his job description.

   - My next step is to meet with WM on her performance goals for the third quarter.

Appendix C

SAMPLE 24 FORM

In The Accountability System, "24" refers to the 24 hours right before the next coaching session. Like the 48, the 24 report has two primary parts: (1) play back what was accomplished (or not accomplished) since the last session; and (2) play forward what the employee would like to talk about in the upcoming coaching session.

Below is a sample 24 coaching prep form that you can use as-is, or customize to your situation. You can download this form at www.tandem-partners.com.

ACCOUNTABILITY COACHING
"24" PREP FORM

To get the most from our next accountability coaching session, please respond to the questions below and return to me at least 24 hours prior to our scheduled session.

Name: _____ Session Date: _____

1. Accomplishments and progress made since our last coaching session:
   _____
   _____

2. Commitments I made in our last coaching session:
   _____
   _____

3. What happened around those commitments:
   _____
   _____

4. Challenges I'm facing right now:
   _____
   _____

5. Opportunities available to me right now:
   _____
   _____

6. What I want to focus on in our next coaching session:
   _____
   _____

C.L.E.A.R. COACHING AGENDA **Employee:** Adam Kreg

Progress Report for Managers
Your performance is based on the performance of your people.

Coaching Check-Ins and Ratings (On a scale of 1 – 10)	For the Coaching Session Dated:						
	7/14	7/28	8/13	8/30	9/14	9/27	
Your General Status (Coachee):	8	8	9	9	5	8	
Our Relationship (Coach and Coachee):	8	8	8	7	8	8	
Jim Performance/Development	6 / 9	6 / 9	7 / 9	7 / 8	7 / 9	8 / 9	
Tommy Performance/Development	9 / 8	9 / 9	9 / 8	9 / 8	9 / 8	9 / 8	
Sarah Performance/Development	6 / 2	5 / 2	4 / 2	4 / 1			
Penny Performance/Development	8 / 7	7 / 8	8 / 8	7 / 7	8 / 7	8 / 7	
Zach Performance/Development	8 / 7	8 / 8	8 / 8	8 / 8	9 / 8	9 / 8	
Michael Performance/Development	7 / 7	7 / 7	6 / 7	6 / 7	7 / 8	7 / 8	

Agenda/Level of Consciousness
Clarify the goals for the coaching session • Link back to prior coaching sessions

(Source Documents: Assessments, Performance Reviews, 360 Feedback, Coaching Sessions, 48/24, etc.)

Coaching Areas of Focus and Ratings (On a scale of 1 – 10)	For the Coaching Session Dated:						
	7/14	7/28	8/13	8/30	9/14	9/27	
#1: Budget management skills	6	6	5	7	7	7	
#2: Build stronger business network	7	7	3	7	8	8	
#3: Working with JD toward next promotion	7	7	9	8	8	9	
#4: Being consistently early/on time	5	5	5	6	8	8	
#5: Not over-committing		7	9	5	9	9	
#6: Relationship with peers				6	6	7	
#7:							
#8:							

◆——— **What's the Evidence?** ———◆

Appendix E

SAMPLE UPFRONT AGREEMENTS

On the next few pages, you'll find four sample Upfront Agreements. These are actual agreements my clients have used (and in most cases, continue to use) with the people they're coaching. These agreements have been modified slightly to maintain confidentiality.

Note the variety of styles in these documents. Also note that people sometimes define Upfront Agreement in their own words at the top.

Some of the same language echoes across these documents; that's because they may have been influenced by other samples I provided. That's fine—that's what samples are for. Don't feel a need to reinvent the wheel if some of this language suits you, too.

Some of the language may not be entirely clear to an outsider. Sometimes, you can't tell right away who the writers mean by "I" or "you." I intentionally left that unexplained as a way to illustrate that these are personal documents, not legal ones. They only have to make sense to the two people involved. If you and person you're coaching know who the "I" and "you" represent in your Upfront Agreement, that's all you need.

These documents can be finalized by the coach-manager or the person being coached, but of course, should be drafted and reviewed together first.

Upfront Agreement – Sample #1

An Upfront Agreement, in a coaching relationship, is communication about how we're going to work together going forward in our sessions. It's important to set the stage in the beginning of this new relationship so we both understand what's expected. The Upfront Agreement is a living document. We can each add and subtract components as we see necessary in the success of our relationship.

Components of Our Upfront Agreement

- **What we need for a successful relationship**: Open communication, equality, environment to be honest with each other, candidness, and respectfulness.

- **Permission to say or do certain things**: My intention is to take off my manager hat and put on my coaching hat. I want you to know that it's okay to be open and honest. It's also okay not to know all the answers.

- **Personal communication statement**: For both of us: reciprocal, respectful, not condescending, honest. "The quickest way to resolve anything is through the truth."

- **Coaching you best**: It's important to know that people like to be coached in different ways. You need to be able to tell me how you want to be coached throughout our sessions.

- **My goal**: What I want for you is what you want for you.

- **My intention**: To open the door for you to say what's on your mind without your having to fear retribution. To achieve that, I am committed to listening first and not reacting, and to asking for more information rather than getting defensive.

- **Our responsibilities**: Start and end on time. Show up for our sessions. My responsibility to you is to support your goals and help break down barriers to your success. Your responsibility is to use the coaching sessions to help you achieve your goals and to do the necessary activities to achieve your goals.

- **Consequences**: These sessions are all about YOU. There are no consequences except that the likelihood of achieving your goals will be diminished if you're not committed.

- **Timeframes**: Your particular time is set in stone with my schedule. If you have a problem with attending at that time, just tell me. The sessions will last one hour, ending and starting on time. There will be no interruptions.

- **Agenda**: You set the agenda. It's your goal and your meeting. I'm there to support and help you.

- **48/24**: This is important to your coaching success. 48 means giving me an email recap of our session, within 48 hours, showing what we talked about and what you plan to do between the last session and the next session. 24 means sending me an email 24 hours ahead of our next scheduled meeting, showing me what you've accomplished toward your goal and what you want to talk about in our session. 48/24 should be short, bulleted and to the point. It's meant to help you clarify what we talked about, what you expect from me, and vice versa.

- **Confidential!** All sessions are completely confidential. What is said behind doors remains behind doors.

- **Request**: I will make requests of you in our sessions that are related to achieving your goals. These requests are not mandatory but may be essential if you want to achieve your goals. My intention with the word request is to remind you that it's optional, and that we can discuss and modify the request based on your feedback.

- **Back on track**: It's okay to get off track every now and then if you have something that's on your mind and you need to talk about it, even if it's not related to your goal. At the same time, if we wander too far off track, both of us have permission to request that we get "back on track" when we feel the necessity.

- **Taking notes**: Both of us have the permission to take notes during the sessions to make sure we have clarity on what's being said and who will perform certain tasks, etc.

- **This is new!** The Accountability System is new for both you and me, so it's okay to make mistakes, acknowledge them, and learn together.

I consider these sessions the most important task I do all week. It's my chance to offer support and help in achieving your goals here at XYZ Company. I look forward to our continued relationship and success.

_____

Coach -Manager

_____

Employee

_____

Date

Upfront Agreement – Sample #2

The intention of this agreement is to create an understanding between you and me about what we expect from each other.

It is an agreement about how we will work together going forward.

It is an agreement that we make about responsibilities, expectations, and communication.

It is my intention to give you the support you need to achieve your goals within this company, and also your career goals.

GROUND RULES

Meeting Times

- Meetings will be held every two weeks.
- All meetings will start and stop at the designated times.

Communication

- It is my intention to create an atmosphere of open and honest communication. I would like you to say what is on your mind, as will I.

- It is not in our mutual best interest to use our time together to complain about people or situations. Rather, we should focus on specific goals and problems and finding the best solutions to those problems.

- We will agree to focus our attention on the specific topics of our meetings and if anyone should stray from those topics and become engaged in "storytelling," the other person will have the right to stop them to return to the original topic.

- We will always discuss what is positive and what exceeds our agreed upon standards as well as commenting on anything that is not meeting standards.

- Two differences we want to be aware of:

- _____ prefers to see an email before having a discussion about a topic. _____ prefers NOT to be asked for opinions via email or other writing, and requests in-person or phone conversations instead.

- _____ doesn't like to dance around things: "Just give it to me straight." _____ requests some "gift-wrapping," along the lines of "here are three things you're doing well," before hearing criticism.

Requests

- I will make requests of you in our sessions that are related to achieving your goals. These requests and the subsequent action required are optional and open for discussion.

- You can also make requests of me—for instance, to complete a task that can help you achieve specific goals.

Support of Other Managers

From time to time, other managers may come to you for information or assistance that is needed to achieve their department's specific goals. It is expected that in the spirit of successful teamwork, you will make every effort to supply other managers with the help and assistance that is requested.

My Expectations of You

- That you will work in a consistent manner to achieve the goals that you have set.

- If we agree that these goals are not being met or something is not meeting our standards, you will help to identify the source of the problem and we will work together to remove the problems or reset new goals.

Your Expectations of Me

- That I will supply the support and resources you need to achieve your goals.

- If you do not feel that you are receiving the support and resources that are needed, you have the right to speak openly and honestly about the situation.

When There Is a Problem between You and Someone Else

- My commitment is to approach each case with the assumption that I have heard only part of the story. I will probe you for information and I will sometimes ask the same questions the other person asks if I think they're legitimate questions. That doesn't mean I agree with the other person.

- You should expect that I will follow up and ask if the person talked with you; I will want to know what happened. This is like your following up with an XYZ customer service call. It doesn't mean I don't trust you or that I agree with the other person; it means I'm curious and want to know the outcome of the conversation.

- I will commit to asking you these kinds of questions in private.

I have read the preceding **Upfront Agreement** and am willing to work to the best of my ability to commit my time, talent and effort to meeting the goals and expectations of my department and XYZ Company.

_____

President, XYZ Company

_____

Sales Manager, XYZ Company

_____

Date

SAMPLE UPFRONT AGREEMENT #3

This agreement is all about you achieving your career goals—through open and safe communication, where we both listen carefully and try not to take things personally. To do so, I need to understand your professional goals and how you would define success in your role here. Your goals and your success need to be aligned with what is in the best interest of the ABC organization.

1. You have my permission to be open and honest.

2. Our communication will be reciprocal, respectful and honest and without fear of retribution.

3. We need to ensure I understand your communication style.

4. My feedback will focus on your work and goals and will always be constructive.

5. For _____, it's very important to finish sentences before the other person speaks. Please don't jump in when there are pregnant pauses—just wait. That will ensure a feeling of "being heard."

6. I will request your commitment to certain actions—though not mandatory, they may be essential to you achieving your goals.

7. I expect that when something doesn't meet our standards, you will address it and keep me informed.

8. Weekly meeting format:

   • Regularly scheduled meeting (begin and end on time; neutral place).

   • Recap at the end of the meeting to confirm *your commitment* to what is to be done over the next week (which may need to be confirmed in an email from you).

   • Prior to each weekly meeting, you will send an email outlining what commitments have been accomplished.

- Where items have not progressed, please note what is stopping and blocking you; what will help you moving forward.
- At the beginning of each meeting, we will revisit the prior week's recap and committed actions.

_____

Coach -Manager

_____

Employee

_____

Date

Sample Upfront Agreement #4

The following agreement is between _____ and _____
_____ and is intended to outline an understanding of how each of
us will interact with the other under The Accountability System.
It is an understanding about what we expect from each other and a
description of how we will work together from now on. It covers
responsibilities, expectations, and our communication styles.

As a supervisor, _____'s intention is to help _____
achieve his business goals, obtaining the results he desires and
that the company needs from him.

When we talked about defining success, we developed a set of
baseline and goal performance targets that, for the most part, are
captured in _____'s individual development plan.

While there are many areas that are measured, the key drivers to
performance for _____ boil down into three key measurements:

- Number of new leads obtained
- Number of sales made
- Gross margin

All other measurements and personal growth and development
activities drive toward the attainment of specific levels of performance in each of those three categories.

In order to assist _____ achieve his results, we agree to the
following:

1. Permission to say or do certain things. For the most part, we
    agree that we should take off our respective manager and em-
    ployee hats and put on our team member collaboration hats.
    We agree that we will be open and honest with each other, and
    admit what we don't know. _____ agrees to invoke su-
    pervisory authority only when absolutely necessary. We agree

that we can bring up any subject—anything at all—that we think might be relevant to our work together. We commit to doing so without belittling each other or making each other feel wrong.

2. We agree to make our communication reciprocal, respectful, not condescending, and honest.

3. We agree that as we move forward on this new style of interacting, we will adjust this agreement and our interaction style as we agree it will best serve us.

4. _____'s intention is to open the door to say openly and honestly what's on our minds without _____ having to fear retribution. To do that, _____ is committed to listening first and not reacting, and to asking for more information rather than getting defensive.

5. If we say something that was not intended or that comes out the wrong way, we agree to correct it and apologize to the other if appropriate.

6. We acknowledge that sometimes we just need to vent. We agree that when doing so, we will declare upfront that it's coming. We agree to vent only as long as necessary to relieve oneself and to get back on track.

7. We agree that personal issues and matters are fair game for discussion, particularly as they relate to or impact our ability to focus and perform and work.

8. In giving feedback, _____ will focus on the work, not the person who created the work. _____ agrees to discuss what is positive and what exceeds our agreed-upon standards as well as commenting on anything that doesn't meet the standards. The focus will be on constructive ways to bring actual results in line with standards.

9. We acknowledge that in business there are only three things we truly control and they are our own thoughts, words and actions. We agree to manage these three things for ourselves in ways that support us to achieve our desired results.

- We acknowledge that our thoughts drive our emotions and state of mind, and that our state of mind affects how we come across to the world and the people we interact with.

- We further acknowledge that the words we choose to speak, and the style and tone of delivery of those words, have a great deal to do with our personal success and effectiveness.

- We agree to be conscious and aware of our thoughts and the words we speak, always looking to make adjustments to become even more effective than we already are.

- We agree that our actions (and inactions)—the things we choose to do or not do—have the single biggest impact on our results. We agree that we will continually evaluate and assess the effectiveness of our actions and, where appropriate, change our actions until we get our desired result.

10. A request is a suggestion for action. I will make requests of you in our sessions that I believe are related to achieving your goals. These requests are not mandatory. You may reply with "yes," "no," or "let's discuss."

11. We agree to keep our word with each other. We further agree that in situations where we did not or were not able to keep our word, we will acknowledge that fact, clean up any impact that resulted from not keeping our word, and if appropriate, recommit to do what it was we originally said we would do.

12. We agree each of us is responsible for our own work and we take complete responsibility for our results, good and bad. We will not allow ourselves to blame others or situations for our lack of results. We commit to being resourceful and creative in finding new ways of clearing and defeating obstacles that will lead to the attainment of our desired results.

Appendix F

SUGGESTED CONTENT FOR
UPFRONT AGREEMENTS

The way you craft your Upfront Agreement will depend on who you are, who your employee is, and the very things you'll be talking about: responsibilities, expectations and communication. Some people create the Upfront Agreement in a straightforward fashion, following my guidelines. Others engage in a more free-ranging conversation that ultimately leads to the same result: a clear pact that establishes mutual agreements about how you plan to work together going forward.

I recommend that you take notes during the discussion of your Upfront Agreement, so that afterward, you can convert the notes to paragraph or bullet form. These notes can be kept in your Accountability Binder.

In any case, here are some ideas to get you started. Ask your employee for his or her answers, and at the same time, be forthcoming about your own preferences. Remember, this is all about mutuality and the beginning of an ongoing conversation between the two of you.

Intentions in Our Relationship
Fundamentally, the Upfront Agreement is about your relationship. Experiment with any questions that will point you toward clarifying the kind of relationship you want and hope to have. Here are some good openers:

- *How can I be a good coach-manager for you?*
- *What will enable you to get the most out of our relationship?*
- *In an ideal world, what sort of relationship do you hope we will be able to create?*
- *What else do you think we need in order to create a successful relationship?*

- *What are some of your personal and professional values (education, hard work, love, courage, fairness, loyalty, integrity, etc.)? How might these affect our working relationship?*
- *What are some of your strengths? What are some of mine?*
- *I'd like to encourage you to be open with me, without fear of any sort of retribution. What can I do to assure you that I have your best interests at heart?*

Responsibilities and Expectations

What do you expect from your team members? Don't assume that they know. They also might not know how they will be rewarded for success. Responsibilities might or might not be spelled out in your employees' job descriptions. People may or may not have read those documents recently, and may or may not recall the specifics. Yet accountability can't happen until we clarify expectations.

An Upfront Agreement conversation offers an excellent opportunity to review and clarify the job description and essential responsibilities. A client of mine summed this up by saying, "The Accountability System ensures that you know, that they know, and that you both do it."

- *What are my responsibilities to you as your coach-manager?*
- *What are your responsibilities to me as leader of this team?*
- *What are your responsibilities in your work role?*
- *What are our responsibilities to each other regarding your ability to make your best contributions?*
- *What expectations do you have of yourself that go beyond your essential responsibilities?*

Communication Challenges and Preferences

Clarifying how the two of you will communicate is a key element of the Upfront Agreement. Take time to explore, ask questions and investigate options. When you've got clarity, you and your employee will create a brief Personal Communication

Statement that summarizes your answers to these questions. Your Personal Communication Statement should then be integrated into the Upfront Agreement. (See below for examples.)

- *How does each of us like to receive information? (Written? Verbal? Email?)*
- *How are we most comfortable giving information?*
- *What's important about the way we speak to each other?*
- *Who is responsible for making sure we understand each other?*
- *Are we open to receiving any kind of feedback from each other, as long as it's delivered in a respectful and professional manner?*
- *What will we do if we don't know or don't understand something?*

This last question may seem obvious: if you don't understand, of course you should say so and of course the other person would want you to speak up. But many employees get the impression that "not knowing" is somehow wrong or shameful. So I find it's helpful if this is spelled out in the Upfront Agreement: it's okay not to know. Or, as one of my clients put it, "It's okay not to know—what's **not** okay is if you don't know and you don't let me know."

Sample Personal Communication Statements

A Personal Communication Statement (PCS) describes how you want others to communicate with you. While at first glance it may seem obvious—everyone wants to be treated professionally, and with respect—in fact, individuals have individual preferences, and it's helpful to identify them when you start working together. If you haven't asked this question before—how would you like to communicate with each other?—you may be surprised to find that people do have strong preferences that would not necessarily have occurred to you.

A PCS should be included in your Upfront Agreement. Below are some PCS samples that were generated by my clients. Your PCS might be longer, shorter, or in a different format, but here are some ideas to get you thinking about your own preferences.

As you read these, imagine how these statements might affect your own communication style if these were incorporated into your Upfront Agreement, and you'll begin to see the power of the PCS.

I operate best in an environment where I know the facts, what is expected, and where we're headed. I expect my coworkers to be truthful with me and inform me of mistakes I have made or ways that I can improve.

* * *

I like to use humor when appropriate to lighten the day-to-day tensions. However, I don't like sarcasm or "jokes" that are made at other people's expense.

* * *

I want to have the opportunity to be heard, understood and respected for what I have to contribute. In turn, I will demonstrate a willingness to show consideration and appreciation of others and their points of view.

* * *

I like to communicate in a way that is enthusiastic, positive, and contributes to solving problems. I don't believe complaining or "venting" is a good form of communication.

* * *

In a fast-paced business like ours, there are times when we can be hurtful without meaning to. I will think carefully about the way I present things. I will try not to be overly sensitive to the way you communicate with me, knowing that our styles are very different.

* * *

The main thing I ask is your honesty. Whether it is praise or criticism, good news or bad, the fact that you respect me enough to be truthful is good enough for me.

* * *

Sometimes I need time to respond to questions. I'm not always good at having the answer on the spot. So when we're communicating, I need you to not pressure me for an answer right at that moment. Please give me time to think about things first, so that I can do my best thinking.

* * *

I want my space, lifestyle and personal choices to be respected. I prefer not to talk about personal matters at work. It's not because I'm not a friendly person, I just need you to understand and respect my privacy.

* * *

It is our obligation and our right to bring up any issues that affect our working relationship. Therefore, I agree to bring up issues immediately, or as soon as possible after I experience them, to make sure that I keep my communication clear and my expectations current.

* * *

I will never undermine you, or any of our team members, in front of other people.

* * *

If I'm not living up to my responsibilities, I want you to "call it like it is." I don't want you to shy away from giving me "bad news." It doesn't make me feel better to be in the dark, so don't feel like you have to protect my feelings.

* * *

When there is a problem or conflict, I will not deliver messages for other people and I will not ask anyone to do that for me. I want other people to speak to me directly and listen directly to me.

Permissions and Requests

"Permission" is not a word that's used a lot in a business context. But it can be helpful to ask for and receive permission to do certain things, such as give honest feedback, or admit that one or both of you is uncertain about something—or simply, in the case of some of my clients, permission to take notes during coaching sessions.

While note taking may seem a natural activity in a business meeting, getting permission upfront for coaching sessions can be important. Some people feel like you're not paying attention to them if you're taking notes.

When you ask for permission to take notes, it's an opportunity to explain how the notes will be used: to clarify your agreements, to remind you both of action items, and for other legitimate purposes. In other words, you can explain that note taking actually helps you pay closer attention. Also, by talking about this, you can assuage any fears that the notes might be used against employees, or placed in their personnel files, as people sometimes suspect. And at the end of a coaching session, when you're recapping what's been said and agreed to, the other person will notice that indeed, your note taking came in handy.

- *What would you like permission to do or say with me?*
- *How do you feel about taking notes during our coaching session?*
- *What should we do if our questions get off track, or one of us starts "storytelling"?*
- *What other sorts of requests would we like to make of each other?*
- *What other kinds of permissions would we like to have from each other, or give to each other?*

Commitments and Consequences

Accountability involves making commitments: commitments to the coaching process, the coaching relationship and to actions agreed on in coaching sessions. In an ideal world, we all would live up to all of our commitments all of the time. Of course, we know that it's not always possible, and that we also sometimes fall down. So what's the best way for you and the person you're coaching to handle commitments and the consequences of not fulfilling them? What about rewards? Here are some questions that may prompt your discussion.

- *What should happen if we don't live up to our responsibilities?*
- *What should happen if we don't live up to this Agreement?*
- *What should I do or not do if you get behind on your goals or commitments?*
- *What are your suggestions for a reward system?*
- *What about timelines for fulfilling commitments? Who sets the timeline?*

- *How will each of us benefit if we do live up to our responsibilities, and this Agreement?*

Coaching Session Logistics

In your Upfront Agreement, you may want to address some practical matters, including where, when and how often you'll meet.

- *How do we feel about the recommended one-week interval in between coaching sessions? Do we need to meet every week at first, before moving to bi-weekly?*
- *Where will we meet? What "neutral territory" would work best for us both?*
- *How long will each meeting last?*
- *What about cell phones and other interruptions?*
- *How important is it to start and end on time?*
- *What if one of us can't make a scheduled coaching session? What guideline would we like to put in place about rescheduling?*
- *How would we like to begin each coaching session? What should we do or talk about toward the end of each session?*

Confidentiality

How do the two of you define confidentiality in your coaching relationship? This can vary widely from one relationship to another. Some people feel comfortable discussing just about anything, while others choose to put some boundaries or guidelines in place. Here are some questions to ask.

- *How do you personally define confidentiality? How should we define confidentiality in our coaching relationship?*
- *What issues, if any, are off limits in our discussions?*
- *If the person you're coaching also is coaching others: There may be times when you'd like to discuss one of your employees with me. How will we handle issues of confidentiality in that situation?*
- *If one of us feels that confidentiality has been broken, how should we handle it?*

Techniques and Tools

In this book there are numerous techniques and tools to help you get the most out of your coaching sessions, such as the 48, the 24, recapping, making requests, and more. Of course, you can't expect your team to agree to use those tools or embrace those techniques before they know what they are. So I recommend that you provide some explanation of each item and express your desire to use them in coaching sessions. Then solicit your employee's agreement to trying them out. Notice how the sample phrasing below takes the form of a request, not a demand.

- *What are your thoughts on using the 24? The 48?*
- *The C.L.E.A.R. Coaching Agenda is one structure we could use for conducting coaching sessions. What are your thoughts on that approach?*
- *How about an agreement to use open-ended questions whenever possible?*
- *What are your thoughts on "making requests"?*
- *Using the "recap" technique might help us stay on the same page. What are your thoughts on using recap in our conversations and coaching sessions?*

As you can see, creating an Upfront Agreement is not a five-minute agenda item. Whether you use these proposed questions verbatim, or mix and match with your own, please take time with this process. Don't make it tedious by insisting on an answer to every question listed here, but don't skip over questions just to finish quickly, either.

The point is not only to achieve your end: an Upfront Agreement between you and your employee. The point also is to demonstrate the ACC Model of Accountability: Approach, Care, Clarify. *The way you ask questions, the way you listen to answers, and the way you share your own thoughts and feelings, will send a strong signal to your employee as to what kind of coach-manager you are, or will be.*

Appendix G

POWERFUL, OPEN-ENDED QUESTIONS

Mix and match these powerful, open ended questions to generate productive discussions with your team members.

My All-Time Favorite Question

- What would you like more of or less of in your work life?
- Is there *anything* – personally or professionally – that you want more of?
- What else?
- What else?
- What else?
- Is there *anything* – personally or professionally – that you want less of?
- What else?
- What else?
- What else?

The Three W's

- What does it (your goal or your dream or your success) look like?
- What's in the way?
- What will it take to get there?

Moving to Action through Personal Responsibility

- How do you intend to handle that?
- What's the first step you'll take?
- What next step do you think would be appropriate?
- What's one first step you might take before we meet again?
- What's the path of least resistance in this situation? Is that the best path?
- What advice would you give another person if he or she were in your shoes?
- If you were my coach-manager, how would you coach *me* in this same situation?

- What's stopping you, or blocking you from making this happen?
- What's one thing you could do to change this situation?
- What do you think we should do?
- How do you think we should handle this?
- What are your thoughts on this?
- What do you think would work best?
- Who do you think could be helpful with this?

Establishing a Coaching or Mentoring Relationship

- What's the one thing that would make the biggest difference for you right now?
- What are the three biggest changes you need to make in your work life over the next year?
- What's your most urgent business problem right now?
- What problems seem unsolvable?
- What are the three biggest opportunities you have right now that you're not making the most of?
- What changes will be required for you to make the most of what we've talked about?
- What's the most helpful thing I can do for you during our coaching sessions?
- What single area of focus in our coaching would help you reach multiple goals?
- Other than support and advice, in what other ways can I help you the most?
- What should I do or not do if you get behind on your goals?
- What improvements would you like to make in your work or career? Your professional skills? Your communication? Your leadership?

Ongoing Coaching/Mentoring Sessions

- What do you need most from me today?
- What's the most pressing thing on your mind today that you're willing to share?
- What's the biggest change you're willing to make today?
- What are the three things you're going to do between now and our next coaching session?

General
- What do you see happening here?
- How do you picture that? What does it look like?
- What did you hear in this discussion?
- How do you feel about that?
- So, what's possible here?
- How could you look at this situation differently?

Vision and Future
- What do you see for yourself in the future?
- What do you see for the people around you?
- What's your personal mission and vision?
- What do you *really* want?
- If you knew you couldn't fail, what would you most like to have, accomplish, or work toward?

Work Satisfaction
- What are the five things you spend most of your time doing during your workday?
- What's the most fulfilling (or exciting) aspect of your work?
- What's the most difficult (or stressful) part of your work?
- What are the three biggest "time wasters" in your day? What step could we take to change that?
- What about the people you work with? In what ways do they contribute to your success? If they're not contributing, tell me more about that.
- What conflicts, if any, are you having at work?
- What resources are missing that you feel are necessary for your success?

Personal Satisfaction
- What are you really committed to?
- What do you really want out of your work life? Or life in general?
- What legacy do you want to leave?
- On a scale of 1 to 10, how would you rate the quality of your life today?

- What, if anything, is causing you stress?
- In what area, if any, is your life out of balance?
- What are you tolerating that you would like to stop tolerating?
- What is the best part of you? Why?
- What are the three most important things you've learned about yourself?
- What (or who) is holding you back the most right now, and how?
- What else, if anything, do you feel is important to accomplish in order for your life to be fulfilled and complete?
- What are you currently learning/accepting about yourself?

Energy and Focus
- What motivates you to want to improve and evolve as a person?
- What keeps you up at night?
- What, if any, sources of energy don't really serve you well or are actually unhealthy?
- What is presently consuming your time that you wish you could eliminate?
- What are your three biggest concerns or fears about yourself and your life?
- In what areas are you not as responsible as you'd like to be?
- What habits do you have that you wish to change?

Offering Your Support and Guidance
- How can I help?
- How can I best support you?
- How can I best support you on this particular project?
- How can I best support you right now?
- What would you most like from me right now?
- What kinds of suggestions might I offer you to help you get started?

Committing to a Timeframe
- When will you complete this project/activity?
- What are the interim steps?
- When will you take the first step?

QUICK ORDER FORM

To Order Individual Copies of

The Accountability Factor: The Buck **Starts** Here

- Call Toll Free 1-888-281-5170; or
- Order online at www.tandem-partners.com; or
- Fax order form to 1-620-229-8978; or
- Mail order form to:

> QP Distribution
> RE: The Accountability Factor
> 22167 C Street
> Winfield, Kansas 67156

Number of copies @ $19.95 each . . . . _____

Total. . . . .$ _____

Maryland residents add 5% sales tax. . . . .$ _____

Shipping
U.S. residents add $4.00 for first book;
      add $2.00 for each additional book . . . .$ _____

International residents add $9.00 for first book;
      add $5.00 for each additional book . . . .$ _____

                               TOTAL $ _____

My check or money order for $ _____ is enclosed.
(Make checks/money orders payable to: Tandem Partners)

Please charge my: ❑ Visa   ❑ MasterCard   ❑ American Express

Name _____ Title _____

Company _____

Address _____

City/State/Zip _____

Phone _____ Email _____

Card # _____ Expiration Date _____

Signature _____

For quantity discounts, call 1-866-649-1902, 8:30 a.m .- 5:00 p.m., EST, Monday through Friday.